150
Best-Ever
Cast-Iron Skillet
RECIPES

P9-DMZ-858

Gooseberry Patch

An imprint of Globe Pequot
246 Goose Lane
Guilford, CT 06437

www.gooseberrypatch.com

1•800•854•6673

Copyright 2016, Gooseberry Patch 978-1-62093-210-0

All rights reserved. No part of this book may be reproduced or utilized in any form or by any means, electronic or mechanical, including photocopying and recording, or by any information storage and retrieval system, without permission in writing from the publisher. Printed in Korea.

Do you have a tried & true recipe...

tip, craft or memory that you'd like to see featured in a **Gooseberry Patch** cookbook? Visit our website at **www.gooseberrypatch.com** and follow the easy steps to submit your favorite family recipe. Or send them to us at:

Gooseberry Patch
PO Box 812
Columbus, OH 43216-0812

Don't forget to include the number of servings your recipe makes, plus your name, address, phone number and email address. If we select your recipe, your name will appear right along with it... and you'll receive a **FREE** copy of the book!

Contents

Most recipes in this book can be prepared using a skillet that isn't made of cast iron. If the dish will bake in the oven, though, be sure to choose a skillet with an oven-safe handle.

Shopping for a cast-iron skillet? For family meals, a 9-inch or 10-inch skillet is perfect. A smaller 8-inch skillet is just right for cornbread or dinner for two. An extra-large 15-inch skillet is just right for frying chicken or burgers for the whole gang!

Seasoning is the key to great meals from a cast-iron skillet. It's simple...rub the skillet lightly all over with melted shortening or canola oil. Bake at 350 degrees for an hour, then let it cool completely in the oven.

If the skillet hasn't been used in awhile, re-seasoning will do it good too. Even an old rusty skillet can be restored to usefulness. Use a steel wool pad to scrub off any rusty spots. Wash well and dry thoroughly, then follow the seasoning steps above.

It's fine if a little soap is needed to get your cast-iron skillet clean, but don't leave it soaking in suds. Promptly rinse well and pat dry.

Rise & Shine

Apple-Stuffed French Toast

Treat your family to this delectable French toast, filled with brown sugar-sweetened apples.

3 apples, peeled, cored and cut
   into chunks
1/4 c. brown sugar, packed
cinnamon to taste
2 eggs, beaten

1/2 c. milk
1 t. vanilla extract
8 slices wheat bread
Garnish: maple syrup

In a saucepan, combine apples, brown sugar, cinnamon and a small amount of water. Cover and simmer over medium-low heat for 5 to 10 minutes, until apples are soft; set aside. Meanwhile, in a separate bowl, whisk together eggs, milk and vanilla. Heat a greased cast-iron skillet over medium heat. Quickly dip bread into egg mixture, coating both sides; place in skillet. Cook until golden on both sides. To serve, place one slice of French toast on a plate; top with a scoop of apple mixture and another slice of French toast. Drizzle with maple syrup. Makes 4 servings.

Surprise sleepyheads at breakfast...serve each person a made-to-order omelet in a mini cast-iron skillet. A cheery red bandanna tied around the handle makes a nice big napkin.

Apple-Stuffed French Toast

Old-Fashioned Blueberry Pancakes

Old-Fashioned Blueberry Pancakes

An all-time favorite! Serve with blueberry syrup for a very berry flavor.

2 c. milk
2 eggs, beaten
1/2 c. sour cream
2 c. all-purpose flour
2 T. baking powder

2 T. sugar
1/2 t. salt
1/4 c. oil
1 c. blueberries
Garnish: butter, maple syrup

Combine milk, eggs and sour cream; beat well. In a separate bowl, stir together flour, baking powder, sugar and salt; add to milk mixture. Beat until lumps disappear; mix in oil. Fold in blueberries. Pour batter by 1/4 cupfuls onto a greased, hot cast-iron skillet. Turn when bubbles appear; cook other side. Serve with butter and syrup. Makes 4 to 6 servings.

A chilly morning just seems to call for pancakes! Make lots of 'em in a jiffy. Pour batter into an empty, clean squeeze bottle, ready to squeeze out portions right into a hot skillet.

Breezy Brunch Skillet

*Try this all-in-one breakfast on your next camp-out!
Just set the skillet on a grate over hot coals.*

6 slices bacon, diced
6 c. frozen diced potatoes
3/4 c. green pepper, chopped
1/2 c. onion, chopped

1 t. salt
1/4 t. pepper
4 to 6 eggs
1/2 c. shredded Cheddar cheese

In a large cast-iron skillet over medium-high heat, cook bacon until crisp.
Drain and set aside, reserving 2 tablespoon drippings in skillet. Add
potatoes, green pepper, onion, salt and pepper to drippings. Cook and stir
for 2 minutes. Cover and cook for about 15 minutes, stirring occasionally,
until potatoes are golden and tender. With a spoon, make 4 to 6 wells in
potato mixture. Crack one egg into each well, taking care not to break the
yolks. Cover and cook over low heat for 8 to 10 minutes, until eggs are
completely set. Sprinkle with cheese and crumbled bacon. Serves 4 to 6.

Harriet's Potato Pancakes

*These tender golden pancakes are perfect for breakfast...delicious at
dinner too, garnished with applesauce or sour cream.*

1 c. all-purpose flour
2 t. baking powder
1 t. salt
2 eggs, beaten
1 c. milk

2 T. onion, grated
1/4 c. butter, melted and slightly
    cooled
3 c. potatoes, peeled and finely
    grated

In a small bowl, mix together flour, baking powder and salt; set aside. In a
separate bowl, combine remaining ingredients; mix well. Stir flour mixture
into potato mixture until well blended. Drop by tablespoonfuls onto a
buttered cast-iron skillet over medium heat. Cook on both sides until
golden. Makes 6 servings.

Breezy Brunch Skillet

Hashbrown Skillet Omelet

Hashbrown Skillet Omelet

Set out the catsup and hot pepper sauce...everyone can spice up their portion as they like.

1/2 lb. bacon	6 eggs, beaten
2 T. oil	1/4 c. water
3 c. frozen shredded hashbrowns	1 T. fresh parsley, chopped
1-1/2 c. shredded Cheddar or Cheddar Jack cheese, divided	1/2 t. paprika

Cook bacon in a cast-iron skillet over medium-high heat until crisp. Remove bacon to paper towels. Drain skillet; add oil to skillet. Add frozen hashbrowns and cook without turning for about 10 minutes, until golden. Turn carefully; cook other side until golden. Remove skillet from heat. Sprinkle hashbrowns with crumbled bacon and one cup shredded cheese. Beat eggs and water; pour over cheese. Sprinkle with parsley and paprika. Transfer skillet to oven. Bake, uncovered, at 350 degrees for about 20 to 25 minutes, until eggs are set in the center. Remove from oven; sprinkle with remaining cheese and let stand for 5 minutes. Cut into wedges. Serves 6.

13

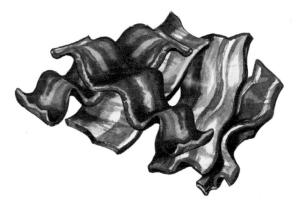

Prepare lots of crispy bacon easily...bake it in the oven! Place bacon slices on a broiler pan, place the pan in a cool oven and turn the temperature to 400 degrees. Bake for 12 to 15 minutes, turn bacon over and bake for another 8 to 10 minutes.

Hashbrown Quiche

A hearty quiche baked in a crust of hashbrowns! Enjoy it for breakfast, or add a zesty salad and have breakfast for dinner.

3 c. frozen shredded hashbrowns, thawed
1/4 c. butter, melted
3 eggs, beaten
1 c. half-and-half

3/4 c. cooked ham, diced
1/2 c. green onions, chopped
1 c. shredded Cheddar cheese
salt and pepper to taste

In a cast-iron skillet, combine hashbrowns and butter. Press hashbrowns into the bottom and up the sides of skillet. Transfer skillet to oven. Bake, uncovered, at 450 degrees for 20 to 25 minutes, until crisp and golden. Remove from oven; cool slightly. Combine remaining ingredients in a bowl; pour mixture over hashbrowns. Reduce oven temperature to 350 degrees. Bake for another 30 minutes, or until quiche is golden and set. Serves 4 to 6.

14

Whip up a holder for a hot skillet handle in a jiffy. Choose a colorful quilted cotton potholder, fold it over and hand-stitch the edges together, leaving one end unsewn. So simple, you'll want to make several.

Hashbrown Quiche

Huevos Rancheros to Go-Go

Rise & Shine

Huevos Rancheros to Go-Go

Serve these eggs with sliced fresh avocado for a deliciously different breakfast.

2 c. green tomatillo salsa
4 eggs
1-1/2 c. shredded Monterey Jack
   cheese

4 8-inch corn tortillas

Lightly grease a cast-iron skillet; place over medium heat. Pour salsa into skillet; bring to a simmer. With a spoon, make 4 wells in salsa. Crack an egg into each well, taking care not to break the yolks. Reduce heat to low; cover and poach eggs for 3 minutes. Remove skillet from heat and top eggs with cheese. Transfer each egg and a scoop of salsa to a tortilla; roll up. Makes 4 servings.

Justin's Skillet Breakfast

Sausage, hashbrowns, chiles and cheese... there's no boring breakfast here!

1/2 lb. ground pork sausage
2 c. frozen shredded hashbrowns
10-oz. can diced tomatoes with
   green chiles, drained

8-oz. pkg. pasteurized process
   cheese spread, diced
6 eggs, beaten
2 T. water

Brown sausage in a large cast-iron skillet over medium heat; drain. Add hashbrowns and tomatoes. Cook for 5 minutes; sprinkle with cheese. Beat eggs with water; pour evenly into skillet. Reduce heat to low; cover and cook for 10 to 12 minutes, until eggs are set in center and cheese is melted. Uncover; let stand 5 minutes before cutting into wedges. Makes 6 servings.

Breakfast Burritos

So versatile! Try substituting leftover shredded chicken or pork for the sausage for another tasty way.

16-oz. pkg. ground pork sausage
8-oz. pkg. shredded Mexican-blend cheese
10-oz. can diced tomatoes with green chiles
5 eggs, beaten
8 10-inch flour tortillas

Brown sausage in a cast-iron skillet over medium heat; drain. In a bowl, combine sausage, cheese and tomatoes; set aside. Add eggs to skillet; scramble as desired. Add scrambled eggs to sausage mixture; mix well. Divide mixture evenly among tortillas and roll up tightly. Wipe skillet clean; grease lightly. Seal tortillas by cooking on hot skillet, seam-side-down, for one to 2 minutes. Makes 8 servings.

Serve Breakfast Burritos in flavorful wraps for a tasty change. There are so many flavors that pair up perfectly with eggs...try spinach, tomato-basil and salsa.

Breakfast Burritos

Farmhouse Sausage Patties

Farmhouse Sausage Patties

*Spice 'em just the way your family likes! Serve alongside
scrambled eggs and hashbrowns.*

1 lb. ground pork
1 t. ground cumin
1/2 t. dried thyme
1/2 t. dried sage

1 t. salt
1/2 t. pepper
Optional: 1/8 t. cayenne pepper

Combine all ingredients; mix well. Cover and refrigerate overnight to allow
flavors to blend. Form into 6 patties. Arrange in a lightly greased cast-iron
skillet and brown both sides over medium heat. Serves 6.

Sawmill Sausage Gravy

*Good gravy! Serve over warm fresh-baked biscuits for a stick-to-your-ribs
breakfast that's sure to please hearty appetites.*

1 lb. ground pork sausage, formed
    into patties
2 T. all-purpose flour

1-1/2 c. milk
salt and pepper to taste

In a cast-iron skillet over medium heat, brown sausage patties. Remove
patties to drain on paper towels, reserving drippings in skillet. Add flour to
reserved drippings and stir until browned. Slowly whisk in milk; cook and
stir until smooth and thickened. Thin with hot water, if needed. Crumble
sausage patties into gravy; season with salt and pepper. Makes 3 cups.

Rise & Shine

Kathy's Denver Sandwich

This is our idea of a good breakfast sandwich! Try it with diced ham too.

4 slices bacon, chopped
1 T. onion, chopped
2 T. green pepper, chopped

3 eggs, beaten
1/4 c. shredded Cheddar cheese
6 slices bread, toasted and buttered

In a cast-iron skillet over medium-high heat, cook bacon until partially done but not crisp. Add onion and green pepper; cook until softened. Add eggs and cook to desired doneness. Sprinkle with cheese; cover and let stand until melted. Cut egg mixture into 3 pieces; serve each between 2 slices of toast. Makes 3 servings.

Breakfast sliders! Stir up your favorite pancake batter and make silver dollar-size pancakes. Sandwich them together with slices of heat & serve sausage. Serve with maple syrup on the side for dipping...yum!

Kathy's Denver Sandwich

Best-Ever Brunch Potatoes

Best-Ever Brunch Potatoes

Eggs, crispy bacon, golden potatoes...just add a basket of fruit muffins and breakfast is served.

8 slices bacon
3 T. olive oil
2-1/2 lbs. redskin potatoes, diced
8 eggs, beaten
1 t. salt

1/2 T. pepper
3/4 c. sour cream French onion dip
3/4 c. shredded sharp Cheddar
  cheese
1/2 c. green onions, chopped

In a cast-iron skillet over medium-high heat, cook bacon until crisp. Remove bacon to paper towels. Drain skillet; add oil and fry potatoes until tender. In a separate lightly greased skillet, scramble eggs until fluffy; season with salt and pepper. Fold crumbled bacon, dip and cheese into potatoes; stir in scrambled eggs. Sprinkle green onions over top. Serves 6 to 8.

Serve poached eggs with breakfast potatoes or hash. Fill a skillet with water and bring to a simmer. Swirl the water with a spoon and gently slide in an egg from a saucer. Let cook until set, about 2 minutes, and remove egg with a slotted spoon.

Cheese & Chive Scrambled Eggs

Served with bacon and warm biscuits, this dish is so tasty you may want to have it for a quick dinner too.

6 eggs, beaten
1/4 t. lemon pepper
1 T. fresh chives, chopped
1/8 t. garlic salt

1 T. butter
1/3 c. shredded Colby Jack cheese
1/3 c. cream cheese, softened

In a bowl, combine eggs, pepper, chives and salt; set aside. Melt butter in a cast-iron skillet over medium-low heat; add egg mixture. Stir to scramble, cooking until set. Remove from heat; stir in cheeses until melted. Serves 2 to 3.

Keep fresh herbs flavorful up to a week. Snip off the ends and arrange them in a tall glass with an inch of water. Cover loosely with a plastic bag and place in the fridge.

Cheese & Chive Scrambled Eggs

Fiesta Corn Tortilla Quiche

Fiesta Corn Tortilla Quiche

Use hot or mild sausage...the choice is up to you.

1 lb. ground pork sausage
5 6-inch corn tortillas
4-oz. can chopped green chiles, drained
1 c. shredded Monterey Jack cheese

1 c. shredded Cheddar cheese
6 eggs, beaten
1/2 c. whipping cream
1/2 c. small-curd cottage cheese

Brown sausage in a cast-iron skillet over medium heat; drain. Set sausage aside; wipe skillet clean. Arrange tortillas in the same skillet, overlapping on the bottom and extending up the sides. Spoon sausage, chiles and cheeses into tortilla-lined skillet. In a bowl, beat together remaining ingredients. Pour egg mixture over sausage mixture. Transfer skillet to oven. Bake, uncovered, at 375 degrees for 45 minutes, or until golden. Cut into wedges to serve. Serves 4.

29

A simple fruit salad goes well with savory breakfast dishes. Cut seasonal fruit into bite-size pieces. Toss with a little poppy seed dressing and add a sprinkle of chopped fresh mint.

Toasted Pecan Pancakes

These very special little pancakes make an
ordinary weekend breakfast extraordinary.

2 eggs, beaten
2 T. sugar
1/4 c. butter, melted and cooled
   slightly
1/4 c. maple syrup
1-1/2 c. all-purpose flour

2 t. baking powder
1/2 t. salt
1-1/2 c. milk
2/3 c. chopped toasted pecans
Garnish: additional maple syrup,
   warmed

In a large bowl, whisk together eggs, sugar, butter and syrup. In a separate bowl, mix together flour, baking powder and salt. Add flour mixture and milk alternately to egg mixture, beginning and ending with flour mixture. Stir in pecans. Set a cast-iron skillet over medium heat and brush lightly with oil. Skillet is ready when a few drops of water sizzle when sprinkled on the surface. Pour batter by scant 1/4 cupfuls onto griddle. Cook until bubbles appear on tops of pancakes and bottoms are golden, about 2 minutes. Turn and cook until golden on the other side, about one minute more. Add a little more oil to griddle for each batch. Serve pancakes with warm maple syrup. Makes about 1-1/2 dozen.

Custardy French Toast

The best French toast you'll ever make! Sit back and enjoy all the compliments.

6 eggs, beaten
3/4 c. whipping cream
3/4 c. milk
1/4 c. sugar

1/4 t. cinnamon
1 loaf French bread, thickly sliced
2 T. butter, divided
Optional: powdered sugar

In a large shallow bowl, whisk eggs, cream, milk, sugar and cinnamon until well blended. Dip bread slices one at a time into egg mixture, turning to allow both sides to absorb mixture. Melt one tablespoon butter in a cast-iron skillet over medium heat. Cook for about 4 minutes per side, until golden and firm to the touch. Repeat with remaining butter and bread. Dust with powdered sugar, if desired. Serves 6 to 8.

Toasted Pecan Pancakes

Nutty Skillet Granola

Nutty Skillet Granola

Fill small bags with this easy-to-fix granola...perfect for grab & go breakfasts and snacks.

1 c. quick-cooking oats, uncooked
1 c. old-fashioned oats, uncooked
1 c. sliced almonds
1/2 c. chopped walnuts
1/2 c. chopped pecans

1/2 c. wheat germ
1/4 c. oil
1/2 c. maple syrup
3/4 c. light brown sugar, packed
1 c. raisins

In a large bowl, mix oats, nuts and wheat germ; set aside. In a large cast-iron skillet over medium heat, combine oil, maple syrup and brown sugar. Cook, stirring constantly, until brown sugar melts and mixture just begins to bubble, about 3 minutes. Add oat mixture; stir well to coat completely. Reduce heat to medium-low. Cook, stirring occasionally, until mixture begins to sizzle and toast, about 3 to 4 minutes; be careful not to burn. Remove from heat; stir in raisins. Cool for 10 minutes; transfer to an airtight container. Will keep for up to 2 weeks. Makes about 7 cups.

33

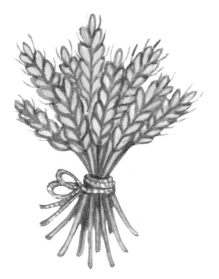

Easy-to-tote snacks like Nutty Skillet Granola are a perfect take-along while visiting the farmers' market, barn sale or auction.

Grandma's Warm Breakfast Fruit

Keep this delectable fruit compote warm for brunch in a mini slow cooker.

3 apples, peeled, cored and thickly
   sliced
1 orange, peeled and sectioned
3/4 c. raisins
1/2 c. dried plums, chopped

3 c. plus 3 T. water, divided
1/2 c. sugar
1/2 t. cinnamon
2 T. cornstarch
Garnish: favorite granola

Combine fruit and 3 cups water in a cast-iron skillet over medium heat. Bring to a boil; reduce heat and simmer for 10 minutes. Stir in sugar and cinnamon. In a small bowl, mix together cornstarch and remaining water; stir into fruit mixture. Bring to a boil, stirring constantly; cook and stir for 2 minutes. Spoon into bowls; top with granola to serve. Serves 6 to 8.

Skillet Strawberry Jam

*Try your hand at jam-making with this simple recipe...
your family will be so pleased, and so will you!*

4 c. strawberries, hulled and
   crushed
1/2 c. sugar

1 T. lemon juice
Optional: 1/4 t. vanilla extract

Combine strawberries, sugar and lemon juice in a cast-iron skillet over medium-high heat; mix well. Cook, stirring often, until strawberries soften and mixture thickens, about 10 minutes. Remove from heat; stir in vanilla, if using. Store in an airtight jar in refrigerator for up to 3 weeks. Makes about 1-1/2 cups.

Have a breakfast get-together for friends & neighbors. Serve pancakes, juices and fruit, then send everyone home with jars of Skillet Strawberry Jam...how neighborly!

Grandma's Warm Breakfast Fruit

Puffy Pear Pancake

Puffy Pear Pancake

*Top each slice of this oven-baked pancake with a
sprinkle of powdered sugar...yum!*

3 eggs, beaten
1 c. milk
1 t. vanilla extract
1 c. all-purpose flour
3 T. sugar

1/4 t. salt
4 pears, peeled, cored and sliced
1/4 c. brown sugar, packed
1/4 c. lemon juice

In a large bowl, whisk together eggs and milk. Add vanilla, flour, sugar and
salt; whisk to combine. Pour batter into a lightly greased large cast-iron
skillet. Transfer skillet to oven. Bake, uncovered, at 425 degrees until
golden and puffy, about 25 minutes. Meanwhile, combine pears, brown
sugar and lemon juice in a bowl; stir well. Pour into a separate skillet or
saucepan over medium heat; sauté until pears are golden, about 5 minutes.
Remove from heat. To serve, spoon warm pear mixture over pancake; cut
into wedges. Serves 4.

37

Ask family & friends to share a copy of tried & true recipe favorites and
create a special cookbook...a great gift for a new cook in the family.

It's always best to use oil or shortening when cooking in cast iron, since non-stick vegetable spray tends to form a sticky, hard-to-remove coating. Bacon drippings work well too...in fact, every time you fry up a skillet of bacon, you're re-seasoning it!

Make crispy potato pancakes with extra mashed potatoes. Stir an egg yolk and some minced onion into 2 cups cold mashed potatoes. Form into patties, dust with a little flour and pan-fry in a little oil until golden.

Invite new neighbors to share a hearty breakfast with you! Send them home with a gift basket filled with flyers from favorite bakeries and pizza parlors, coupons and local maps.

Extra waffles and pancakes can be frozen in plastic freezer bags for up to a month. Reheat them in a toaster for a hearty, quick weekday breakfast.

Sandwiches
& More

Toasted Ham & Cheese

Serve these buttery sandwiches with a side of potato chips and a crisp dill pickle, or a cup of tomato bisque...pure comfort!

2-1/2 T. butter, softened
8 slices sourdough bread
4 slices Colby cheese

1/2 lb. shaved deli ham
4 slices Swiss cheese

Spread butter on one side of each slice of bread. Arrange 4 bread slices, buttered-side down, in a cast-iron skillet over medium-high heat. Top with one slice Colby cheese, desired amount of ham and one slice Swiss cheese. Add remaining bread slices, buttered-side up. Grill sandwiches on both sides until golden and cheese melts. Serves 4.

A budget-friendly tip! The crispiest, tastiest grilled cheese sandwiches start with day-old bread, not super-soft fresh bread.

Toasted Ham & Cheese

Pulled Chicken & Slaw Sandwiches

Sandwiches & More

Pulled Chicken & Slaw Sandwiches

Start with a roast chicken from the deli and you'll be serving these sandwiches in no time! The creamy slaw adds a nice crunch!

1 c. favorite barbecue sauce
1 c. catsup
1/2 c. water
1 t. lemon juice
2/3 c. brown sugar, packed

1 deli roast chicken, boned and
  shredded
6 to 8 buns, split
Garnish: deli coleslaw

In a cast-iron skillet over medium heat, combine barbecue sauce, catsup, water, lemon juice and brown sugar. Stir well; cook and stir until brown sugar is dissolved. Add chicken; reduce heat to low and simmer until mixture is heated through. To serve, spoon chicken mixture onto buns; top with a scoop of coleslaw. Makes 6 to 8 servings.

Quick "pickled" red onions for salads and sandwiches are less pungent than plain raw onions. Cut off the ends of a red onion, cut in half and slice thinly. In a bowl, sprinkle onion with 1/2 teaspoon salt and toss to mix. Let stand 15 minutes and serve. Refrigerate up to 2 days.

Reuben Sandwich

Everyone's favorite deli sandwich!

3 slices deli corned beef
1 to 2 slices Swiss cheese
2 slices pumpernickel or dark rye
   bread

1/4 c. sauerkraut, well drained
1-1/2 T. Thousand Island salad
   dressing
3 T. butter

Arrange corned beef and cheese on one slice of bread. Heap with sauerkraut; drizzle with salad dressing. Add second bread slice. Melt butter in a cast-iron skillet over medium heat. Add sandwich; grill on both sides until golden and cheese melts. Makes one sandwich.

Mom's Salmon Patties

Keep canned salmon on hand to whip up this old-fashioned recipe anytime.

14-3/4 oz. can salmon, drained
   and flaked
1/4 c. onion, finely chopped
1/4 c. cornmeal
1/4 c. all-purpose flour

1 egg, beaten
3 T. mayonnaise
salt and pepper to taste
2 T. oil
4 to 5 sandwich buns, split

Combine all ingredients except oil and buns. Mix until well blended; form into 4 to 5 patties. Heat oil in a cast-iron skillet over medium heat. Add patties and cook until golden on each side, turning only once as patties are fragile. Drain on paper towels. Serve on buns. Makes 4 to 5 servings.

Pick up a stack of vintage-style plastic burger baskets. Lined with paper napkins, they're fun for serving sandwich meals. Clean-up is a snap too...just toss the napkins.

Reuben Sandwich

Creamy Tuna Melts

Creamy Tuna Melts

*These open-faced sandwiches are so warm and cozy after
an afternoon of sledding or skating.*

2 to 3 stalks celery, diced
1 onion, diced
12-oz. can tuna, drained
1/2 c. cottage cheese
1/2 c. mayonnaise

1/4 t. garlic salt
1/8 t. sugar
4 English muffins, split and toasted
8 slices American cheese

In a lightly greased cast-iron skillet, sauté celery and onion until tender.
Add tuna, cottage cheese, mayonnaise, garlic salt and sugar to skillet. Mix
well, breaking up tuna. Cook over low heat until warmed through, stirring
frequently. Remove from heat. Place toasted muffins cut-side up on a broiler
pan. Spread with tuna mixture; top with cheese slices. Broil until cheese
melts. Makes 8 servings.

47

For the prettiest croutons, cut bread with a small cookie cutter. Brush
cut-outs with olive oil, place on a baking sheet and bake at 350 degrees
until crisp and golden.

Pepper Jack-Crab Bisque

So easy to make, yet simply splendid! Garnish with a drizzle of cream.

2 T. butter
2 stalks celery, finely chopped
1 onion, finely chopped
2   10-3/4 oz. cans tomato bisque
   or tomato soup
2-1/2 c. whipping cream or half-
   and-half

3   8-oz. pkgs. imitation crabmeat,
   flaked
1-1/2 c. finely shredded Pepper
   Jack cheese

Melt butter in a deep cast-iron skillet over medium heat. Add celery and onion; cook until softened. Add bisque or soup, cream or half-and-half and crabmeat. Simmer over low heat until heated through. Stir in cheese until melted. For a thinner consistency, stir in a little more cream or half-and-half as desired. Makes 6 servings.

Grandma's Wilted Lettuce

An old-fashioned favorite! To save time, heat the water, vinegar, sugar, and drippings in a mug in the microwave.

2 heads leaf lettuce, torn
Optional: 1/8 t. salt, 1/8 t. pepper
2 eggs, hard-boiled, peeled and
   quartered
Optional: 2 green onions, sliced

4 to 6 slices bacon
1/4 c. vinegar
2 T. water
1 T. sugar

Arrange lettuce in a salad bowl; season with salt and pepper, if desired. Add eggs and green onions, if using. Toss to combine; set aside. Meanwhile, in a cast-iron skillet over medium-high heat, cook bacon until crisp. Remove bacon to a paper towel; reserve drippings in skillet. Add vinegar, water and sugar to drippings in skillet. Heat to boiling, stirring until sugar dissolves. Pour over salad; toss again. Top with crumbled bacon and serve immediately. Makes 6 servings.

Pepper Jack-Crab Bisque

Scott's Ham & Pear Sandwiches

Sandwiches & More

Scott's Ham & Pear Sandwiches

The spiced butter makes these sweet & savory sandwiches especially crispy and good!

8 slices sourdough bread
4 slices Swiss cheese
3/4 lb. sliced deli ham

15-oz. can pear halves, drained
    and thinly sliced

Spread each slice of bread thinly with Spiced Butter. On each of 4 slices, place one slice of cheese; layer evenly with ham and pears. Top with remaining bread slices and press together gently. Spread outsides of sandwiches with Spiced Butter. Heat a cast-iron skillet over medium-high heat. Add sandwiches; cook until crisp and golden, about 5 minutes on each side. Makes 4 sandwiches.

Spiced Butter:

1/2 c. butter, softened
1 t. pumpkin pie spice
1/2 t. ground coriander

1/2 t. ground ginger
1/2 t. salt

Combine all ingredients until smooth and well blended. Keep refrigerated.

At farmers' markets, watch for heirloom vegetables...varieties that Grandma might have grown in her garden. These veggies don't always look picture-perfect, but their flavor can't be beat. What could be better with a meal made in Grandma's skillet?

Panzanella Salad

This traditional Italian salad is so delicious...a wonderful way to use veggies fresh from the farmers' market.

1/2 loaf Italian bread, cubed
1/4 c. olive oil
salt and pepper to taste
1 red pepper, chopped
1 yellow pepper, chopped
1 orange pepper, chopped
1 cucumber, chopped

1 red onion, chopped
1 pt. cherry or grape tomatoes
1 to 2 T. capers, drained
6 leaves fresh basil, cut into long, thin strips
3/4 c. Italian salad dressing or vinaigrette

In a cast-iron skillet, toss together bread cubes, olive oil, salt and pepper. Cook over medium-high heat, stirring occasionally, until crisp and golden; drain and cool. Combine remaining ingredients in a large salad bowl. Just before serving, add bread cubes; toss to coat. Makes 6 to 8 servings.

Happiness is like a potato salad...when shared with others, it's a picnic!
-Anonymous

Panzanella Salad

Brown Sugar Barbecue Sandwiches

Brown Sugar Barbecue Sandwiches

*Need a meal for the whole soccer team? This recipe is just the thing! It's
quick because there's no need to brown the beef first.*

1 c. water	1 T. chili powder
3/4 c. catsup	2 t. salt
2 T. brown sugar, packed	1 t. pepper
1 onion, chopped	2 lbs. lean ground beef
2 T. mustard	12 sandwich buns, split

In a large cast-iron skillet, mix all ingredients except beef and buns. Bring
to a boil over medium heat. Add uncooked beef, breaking up with a spatula;
simmer for 30 minutes. Spoon onto buns. Makes 12 servings.

55

Brown Sugar Barbecue Sandwiches are so deliciously juicy! To keep that
juice from dripping, wrap individual servings in aluminum foil, then
peel back as they're eaten.

Hug in a Mug Soup

A quick-to-fix family favorite! Serve in big soup mugs with some hearty bread for a very comforting supper.

1 lb. ground turkey
1 T. butter
1 onion, chopped
3 cloves garlic, minced
1 green pepper, chopped
28-oz. can crushed tomatoes
28-oz. can diced tomatoes, drained
16-oz. can navy beans, drained
 and rinsed

16-oz. can kidney beans, drained
 and rinsed
1.35-oz. pkg. onion soup mix
1 T. dried parsley
1 T. dried basil
8 c. water
salt and pepper to taste
1 c. small pasta shells, uncooked

Brown turkey in a large cast-iron skillet over medium heat; drain and set aside. In the same pan, melt butter over medium heat. Sauté onion, garlic and green pepper until tender. Stir in crushed tomatoes with juice and remaining ingredients except pasta. Bring to a boil; stir in uncooked pasta. Simmer, uncovered, over medium heat for 10 minutes, or until pasta is tender. Serves 8.

Pull out your oversize coffee mugs when serving soups, stews and chili 'round the campfire. They're just right for sharing hearty servings, and the handles make them so easy to hold onto.

Hug in a Mug Soup

Skillet-Toasted Corn Salad

Skillet-Toasted Corn Salad

An old country favorite! You'll want to stop by the local farmstand to pick up some fresh sweet corn...just for this salad!

1 T. olive oil
6 ears sweet corn, husked and
    kernels sliced off
4 red, yellow and/or green peppers,
    coarsely chopped

1/2 c. shredded Parmesan cheese
1 head romaine lettuce, cut
    crosswise into 1-inch pieces

Heat oil in a large cast-iron skillet over medium-high heat; add corn kernels. Sauté for 5 minutes, or until corn is tender and golden, stirring often. Remove from heat. Combine warm corn, peppers and cheese in a large salad bowl. Pour Dressing over top; toss lightly to coat. Serve corn mixture warm, spooned over beds of lettuce. Makes 8 servings.

Dressing:

1/3 c. oil
1/3 c. lemon juice
1 T. Worcestershire sauce
3 to 4 dashes hot pepper sauce

3 cloves garlic, minced
1/4 t. salt
1/2 t. pepper

Combine all ingredients in a jar with a tight-fitting lid. Cover and shake well.

Try this tip for easily removing fresh corn kernels from the cob. Set an ear of corn in the center opening of a tube cake pan and run a sharp knife down the ear. The kernels will drop right into the pan.

Chicken Ranch Quesadillas

For an easy-to-handle party snack, slice each quesadilla into 8 mini wedges.

1/2 c. sour cream ranch dip
8 8-inch flour tortillas
1 c. shredded Cheddar cheese
1 c. shredded Monterey Jack cheese

10-oz. can chicken, drained and
  flaked
1/3 c. bacon bits
Optional: salsa

Spread 2 tablespoons dip on each of 4 tortillas. Top each with 1/4 each of the cheeses, chicken and bacon bits. Top with remaining tortillas. Place one tortilla stack in a lightly greased cast-iron skillet. Cook over medium-high heat until lightly golden, pressing down gently with spatula. Turn carefully; cook until cheese is melted. Let stand for 2 minutes; slice into wedges. Repeat with remaining tortilla stacks. Serve with salsa, if desired. Serves 4.

Make a speedy black bean salad to serve with Chicken Ranch Quesadillas. Combine one cup drained and rinsed black beans, 1/2 cup corn, 1/2 cup salsa and 1/4 teaspoon cumin. Chill until serving time... easy and tasty!

Chicken Ranch Quesadillas

Toasted Ravioli

Toasted Ravioli

An unusual snack that's such fun to eat! Try meat-filled ravioli too...it's up to you.

2 T. milk
1 egg
3/4 c. Italian-seasoned dry bread
 crumbs
1/2 t. salt

24 frozen cheese-filled ravioli,
 thawed
oil for deep frying
1 T. grated Parmesan cheese
Garnish: marinara sauce, warmed

Whisk milk and egg together in a small bowl. Place bread crumbs and salt in a separate small bowl. Dip ravioli into milk mixture; roll in crumbs to coat. Pour 2 inches of oil into a deep cast-iron skillet. Heat oil to 375 degrees, until a cube of bread sizzles and turns brown. Add ravioli, a few at a time. Fry for about one minute on each side, until golden. Drain on paper towels; sprinkle with Parmesan cheese. Serve warm with marinara sauce for dipping. Makes 2 dozen.

Pickle-O's

Treat your friends to tasty fried pickles just like your favorite hometown restaurant serves.

2 c. dill pickle slices, drained
2/3 c. all-purpose flour
1/3 c. yellow cornmeal

1 c. buttermilk
oil for deep frying
Garnish: ranch salad dressing

Pat pickle slices dry with paper towels; set aside. In a shallow bowl, combine flour and cornmeal. Add buttermilk to a separate bowl. Dip pickles into buttermilk, then into flour mixture. In a deep cast-iron skillet, heat 2 inches of oil over medium-high heat to 375 degrees. Working in batches, add pickles to hot oil. Fry until golden on both sides, about 3 minutes. Drain on paper towels. Serve warm with ranch salad dressing for dipping. Serves 8.

Thumbs-Up Cornbread Salad

Be sure to get your share early...it'll be gone before you know it! Save time by baking the cornbread ahead of time.

8-1/2 oz. pkg. cornbread mix
24-oz. can pinto beans, drained
   and rinsed
2 15-oz. cans corn, drained
1/4 c. sweet onion, diced
1 c. cherry tomatoes, quartered
1/3 c. celery, chopped

1/2 c. bacon, crisply cooked,
   crumbled and divided
2 c. shredded 4-cheese blend
   cheese, divided
1 c. sour cream
2 c. ranch salad dressing

Prepare and bake cornbread according to package directions; set aside to cool. Crumble cornbread into a large serving bowl. Add beans, corn, onion, tomatoes, celery, 1/4 cup crumbled bacon and 1-1/2 cups cheese. Toss well; set aside. In another bowl, stir together sour cream and salad dressing; drizzle over cornbread mixture and toss to coat. Sprinkle with remaining bacon and cheese. Serves 10.

Carrying a salad to a picnic or potluck? Mix it up in a plastic zipping bag instead of a bowl, seal and set it right in the cooler. No worries about spills or leaks!

Thumbs-Up Cornbread Salad

Fried Green Tomato Biscuits

Fried Green Tomato Biscuits

These southern classics are great for a summertime breakfast or brunch!
Try one with a tall glass of sweet tea.

16-oz. tube refrigerated buttermilk
   biscuits
1/2 lb. bacon
1 c. buttermilk

1-1/2 c. self-rising cornmeal
salt and pepper to taste
2 green tomatoes, thickly sliced
Garnish: mayonnaise

Bake biscuits according to package directions; set aside. In a large cast-iron
skillet over medium-high heat, cook bacon until crisp. Remove bacon to
paper towels; reserve drippings in skillet. Pour buttermilk into a shallow
bowl. Combine cornmeal, salt and pepper on a small plate. Dip tomato slices
into buttermilk and then into cornmeal mixture, until thickly coated on both
sides. Fry tomatoes in reserved drippings over medium-high heat for
4 minutes per side, or until golden. Drain on paper towels. Split biscuits;
spread bottom halves with mayonnaise. Top each with a tomato slice, some
bacon and the top half of biscuit. Serve warm. Makes 8 sandwiches.

67

Keep self-rising flour on hand for quick homemade biscuits. Cut
1/4 cup shortening into 2 cups self-rising flour, then stir in 2/3 cup
milk. Knead dough gently and pat or roll out 1/2-inch thick. Cut out
biscuits, place on a lightly greased baking sheet and bake at
475 degrees for 10 to 12 minutes.

BBQ Turkey Sandwiches

A different way to enjoy leftover roast turkey! We like to dip ruffled potato chips in the savory sauce.

2 T. butter	1 T. brown sugar, packed
1/4 c. onion, chopped	1/2 t. mustard
8-oz. can tomato sauce	1/2 c. water
1 c. catsup	1/8 t. cinnamon
3 T. Worcestershire sauce	4 c. cooked turkey, cubed
3 T. cider vinegar	8 hamburger buns, split

Melt butter in a large cast-iron skillet over medium-high heat. Sauté onion until softened; add remaining ingredients except turkey and buns. Reduce heat to low. Cover and simmer for 30 minutes, stirring occasionally. Increase heat to medium-low; add turkey to skillet. Cover and simmer over medium-low heat for 10 minutes. Serve turkey mixture warm, spooned onto buns. Makes 8 servings.

Hungarian Barbecued Wieners

So easy for kids to serve themselves when they come in from playing outdoors. Happy eating!

2 T. butter	2 T. brown sugar, packed
1 lb. hot dogs	1 T. Worcestershire sauce
1/3 c. green pepper, finely chopped	1 T. vinegar
1/3 c. onion, finely chopped	1 T. mustard
10-3/4 oz. can tomato soup	8 hot dog buns, split

Melt butter in a cast-iron skillet over medium heat. Add hot dogs, green pepper and onion; cook until hot dogs are browned. Stir in remaining ingredients except buns; reduce heat to medium-low. Cover and simmer for 30 minutes, stirring occasionally. Serve hot dogs on buns, topped with some of the sauce from skillet. Makes 8 servings.

BBQ Turkey Sandwiches

Prosciutto, Brie & Apple Panini

Prosciutto, Brie & Apple Panini

Great in chilly weather with a cup of creamy tomato soup.

1/4 c. butter, softened
1 green onion, finely chopped
1/2 t. lemon juice
1/4 t. Dijon mustard
4 slices sourdough bread
3/4 lb. prosciutto or deli ham,
　thinly sliced

1/2 lb. brie cheese, cut into
　4 pieces and rind removed
1 Granny Smith apple, peeled,
　cored and thinly sliced

In a bowl, beat butter until creamy. Stir in onion, lemon juice and mustard until smooth. Spread half the butter mixture on one side of 2 bread slices. Place slices butter-side down in a cast-iron skillet over medium heat. Top with prosciutto or ham, cheese, apple and remaining bread. Spread remaining butter on top slice. Weight sandwich with a smaller skillet or a bacon press, if desired. Cook over medium heat until bread is toasted and cheese is melted. Serve immediately. Makes 2 servings.

71

For a scrumptious new twist when making grilled sandwiches, spread the outside of the bread with mayonnaise instead of butter.

Family-Favorite Pork Tacos

As good as the tacos at your neighborhood Mexican restaurant!

2 t. oil
1 lb. pork tenderloin, cubed
1 t. ground cumin
2 cloves garlic, minced
1 c. green or red salsa
Optional: 1/2 c. fresh cilantro,
   chopped

8 10-inch corn tortillas, warmed
Garnish: shredded lettuce, diced
   tomatoes, sliced avocado,
   sliced black olives, sour cream,
   shredded Cheddar cheese

Heat oil in a cast-iron skillet over medium-high heat; add pork and cumin. Cook until golden on all sides and pork is no longer pink in the center, about 8 to 10 minutes. Add garlic and cook for one minute; drain. Stir in salsa and heat through; stir in cilantro, if using. Using 2 forks, shred pork. Fill warmed tortillas with pork mixture; add toppings as desired. Makes 8 servings.

Let the kids invite a special friend or two home home for dinner. Keep it simple with Family-Favorite Pork Tacos and a crisp salad. A great way to get to know your children's playmates!

Family-Favorite Pork Tacos

Pizzawiches

Sandwiches & More

Pizzawiches

A tasty twist on good ol' Sloppy Joes...kids love these sandwiches!

1 lb. ground beef
1 onion, diced
4-oz. jar sliced mushrooms, drained
16-oz. jar pizza sauce

6 to 8 hamburger or sub buns, split
6 to 8 slices mozzarella cheese
Optional: sliced black olives, pepperoni slices

Brown beef and onion in a cast-iron skillet over medium heat; drain. Add mushrooms and pizza sauce to skillet; heat through. Assemble sandwiches with beef mixture and cheese slices, adding olives and pepperoni if desired. Makes 6 to 8 servings.

Asian Chicken Wraps

You'll be surprised how quickly these chicken wraps go together... and they're so much tastier than fast food!

2 boneless, skinless chicken breasts, cooked and shredded
2/3 c. General Tso's sauce
1/4 c. teriyaki sauce
4   10-inch flour tortillas

10-oz. pkg. romaine and cabbage salad mix
1/2 c. carrot, peeled and shredded
1/4 c. sliced almonds
2 T. chow mein noodles

Combine chicken and sauces in a cast-iron skillet. Cook over medium heat until heated through; remove from heat. Divide ingredients evenly on each tortilla, beginning with salad mix, carrot, chicken mixture, almonds and ending with chow mein noodles. Roll up tortillas burrito-style. Makes 4 servings.

Toast sandwich buns before adding juicy fillings... it only takes a minute and makes such a tasty difference. Buns will drip less too!

Jan's Prize-Winning Chili

Good enough to win a chili cook-off...pass the saltines, please!

1-1/2 lbs. ground beef
1 onion, chopped
1 clove garlic, minced
29-oz. can tomato sauce
28-oz. can diced tomatoes
2 cubes beef bouillon
2 1-1/4 oz. pkgs. chili
   seasoning mix

7-oz. can diced green chiles
16-oz. can pinto beans, drained
   and rinsed
16-oz. can red kidney beans,
   drained and rinsed
Garnish: sour cream, shredded
   Cheddar cheese, minced onion

Brown beef, onion and garlic in a large deep cast-iron skillet over medium heat; drain. Mix together remaining ingredients except garnish; add to beef mixture. Cover and cook over low heat for at least one hour, stirring occasionally. Garnish individual bowls as desired. Makes 10 to 12 servings.

Bake some crisp cornbread sticks...fun to dip in chili! Simply stir up a corn muffin mix, pour into a cast-iron cornstick pan and bake according to package directions.

Jan's Prize-Winning Chili

Nonni's Escarole & Bean Soup

Nonni's Escarole & Bean Soup

A wonderful meal made from the simplest ingredients. Garnish with freshly shredded Parmesan cheese.

2 T. olive oil
3 cloves garlic, minced
2 bunches fresh escarole, cut into
   bite-size pieces
2 15-oz. cans cannellini beans

32-oz. container chicken broth
1/2 c. spaghetti sauce
1/2 t. dried oregano
1/4 t. pepper

Heat oil in a deep cast-iron skillet over medium-low heat. Add garlic and cook until softened, but not browned. Add as much escarole as possible, stirring to wilt. Add remaining escarole in batches. Stir in undrained beans and remaining ingredients; increase heat to high and bring to a boil. Reduce heat to low; simmer for 5 more minutes. Makes 6 to 8 servings.

If canned beans don't agree with you, just drain rinse them before using...you'll be washing away any "tinny" taste too.

Scrumptious Chicken Sandwiches

Tired of the same old chicken breast for dinner? Perk up your family's appetite with these crisp golden chicken sandwiches.

1 egg, beaten
1 c. milk
4 to 6 boneless, skinless chicken
    breasts
1 c. all-purpose flour
2-1/2 T. powdered sugar
1 T. kosher salt

1/2 t. pepper
Optional: 1/8 t. allspice
oil for frying
4 to 6 hamburger buns, split and
    lightly toasted
Garnish: mayonnaise, dill pickle
    slices

Whisk egg and milk together in a large bowl. Add chicken; turn to coat and refrigerate for one hour. In a separate bowl, combine flour, sugar and spices. Working in batches, drain chicken, reserving egg mixture, and lightly dredge in flour mixture. Dip back into egg mixture, then into flour mixture again. In a cast-iron skillet, heat one inch of oil to 375 degrees. Carefully add chicken to hot oil. Fry for 8 to 10 minutes, until done on both sides and juices run clear. Drain chicken on a wire rack. Assemble sandwiches on toasted buns; garnish as desired. Makes 4 to 6 sandwiches.

80

Creamy Potato Soup

Cook up a quick and satisfying soup in a jiffy, using leftover mashed potatoes.

8 slices bacon
1 onion, chopped
10-3/4 oz. can cream of
    chicken soup

1-1/2 c. mashed potatoes
2 c. milk
1/2 t. salt

In a deep cast-iron skillet over medium-high heat, cook bacon until crisp. Remove bacon and set aside, reserving drippings. Sauté onion in drippings; drain well. Stir in soup, mashed potatoes, milk and salt. Crumble in bacon. Simmer over low heat until heated through. Serves 4.

Scrumptious Chicken Sandwiches

Key West Burgers

For a real Key West experience, enjoy these flavorful burgers with a frozen tropical drink!

1 lb. ground beef
3 T. Key lime juice
1/4 c. fresh cilantro, chopped
salt and pepper to taste

Garnish: shredded lettuce
4 hamburger buns, split
   and toasted

In a bowl, combine beef, lime juice, cilantro, salt and pepper. Mix well; form into 4 patties. In a lightly greased large cast-iron skillet, cook patties over medium heat for 6 minutes. Turn over; cover and cook for another 6 minutes, or to desired doneness. Place lettuce on bottom halves of buns; top with patties. Spread bun tops with Creamy Burger Spread; close sandwiches. Serves 4.

Creamy Burger Spread:

8-oz. pkg. cream cheese, softened
8-oz. container sour cream

3 green onion tops, chopped

Combine all ingredients; blend well. Chill for 15 minutes.

Put a new spin on burgers! Swap out the same ol' buns with different types of bread like English muffins, Italian ciabatta or sliced French bread. Pita rounds make sandwiches that are easier for littler hands to hold.

Key West Burgers

Ruth's Swiss Bacon-Onion Dip

Ruth's Swiss Bacon-Onion Dip

A yummy hot appetizer to serve with your favorite snack crackers.

8 slices bacon
8-oz. pkg. cream cheese, softened
1 c. shredded Swiss cheese
1/2 c. mayonnaise

2 T. green onions, chopped
1 c. round buttery crackers,
  crushed

In a cast-iron skillet over medium-high heat, cook bacon until crisp. Remove bacon to paper towels. Drain skillet and wipe clean. Mix cheeses, mayonnaise and onion; spread in same skillet. Top with crumbled bacon and cracker crumbs. Transfer skillet to oven. Bake, uncovered, at 350 degrees for 15 to 20 minutes, until hot and bubbly. Makes 4 cups.

Hot Mushroom Dip

Delicious with crackers, fresh veggies and even cubes of bread.

2-1/2 c. mushrooms, chopped
1/2 c. green onions, chopped
3 to 4 T. butter
2 T. all-purpose flour
1/2 t. paprika
1/4 c. milk

1 c. sour cream, divided
1/2 t. salt
1/2 t. pepper
1/8 t. cayenne pepper
assorted snack crackers

In a cast-iron skillet over medium heat, sauté mushrooms and onions in butter until tender. Stir in flour and paprika; add milk and 1/2 cup sour cream. Cook over low heat, stirring occasionally, until bubbly. Stir in remaining sour cream and seasonings. Serve hot with crackers. Makes about 1-1/2 cups.

Creamy hot dips are twice as tasty with homemade baguette crisps. Thinly slice a French loaf on the diagonal and arrange slices on a baking sheet. Sprinkle with olive oil and garlic powder, then bake at 400 degrees for 12 to 15 minutes.

Caramelized Onion Dip

This scrumptious dip captures the sweet and savory flavors of caramelized onions...and there's plenty to share with friends!

2 T. olive oil
4 onions, diced
salt to taste
3 T. water
1-1/2 c. plain Greek yogurt
1/2 c. sour cream

2 T. lemon juice
1/4 t. cayenne pepper
Garnish: paprika
cut-up carrots, celery, radishes or
    other vegetables

Heat oil in a large cast-iron skillet over medium heat. Add onions; season with salt. Cook and stir until onions are golden and caramelized, about 35 to 40 minutes. Add water. Cook and stir, scraping up any browned bits on the bottom of the skillet. Transfer onion mixture to a bowl; let stand 30 minutes. Mix in remaining ingredients except garnish. Cover and refrigerate for at least one hour to allow flavors to blend. Sprinkle with paprika before serving. Serve with assorted vegetables for dipping. Serves 12.

86

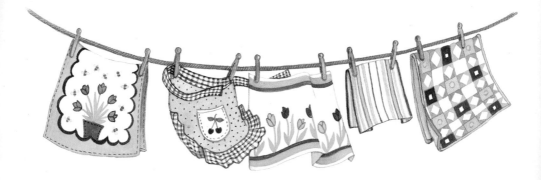

Put out the welcome mat and invite friends over for appetizers...
keep it simple so everyone's free to visit.

Caramelized Onion Dip

Bite-size mini sandwiches make an easy, tasty addition to any casual dinner or party buffet. Whip up some grilled cheese, BLT, Reuben or other favorite sandwiches, then cut them into small squares. Top with an olive or a pickle slice and spear with party picks.

Turn refrigerated dinner rolls into a pull-apart treat at dinnertime. Cut rolls into quarters and place them in a plastic zipping bag with some Parmesan cheese and Italian seasoning. Shake 'em up, pile into a greased skillet and bake as usual.

If you've heard that tomatoes shouldn't be cooked in cast iron, don't worry! Quickly cooked tomato dishes are fine...just avoid long-simmering acidic sauces.

A salt scrub cleans thoroughly while leaving the pan's seasoning intact. Simply scrub the pan with coarse salt and wipe with a soft sponge, then rinse well and pat dry with a soft kitchen towel. It's fine if a little soap is needed to get your cast-iron skillet clean, but don't leave it soaking in suds.

Skillet Meals & Mains

Skillet Bowtie Lasagna

A great hurry-up meal...the pasta cooks right in the skillet!

1 lb. ground beef
1 onion, chopped
1 clove garlic, chopped
14-1/2 oz. can diced tomatoes
1-1/2 c. water
6-oz. can tomato paste

1 T. dried parsley
2 t. dried oregano
1 t. salt
2-1/2 c. bowtie pasta, uncooked
3/4 c. small-curd cottage cheese
1/4 c. grated Parmesan cheese

Brown beef with onion and garlic in a large cast-iron skillet over medium heat; drain. Add tomatoes with juice, water, tomato paste and seasonings; mix well. Stir in uncooked pasta; bring to a boil. Reduce heat to medium-low; cover and simmer for 20 to 25 minutes, until pasta is tender, stirring once. Combine cheeses in a bowl; drop by rounded tablespoonfuls onto pasta mixture. Cover and simmer for 5 minutes. Serves 4.

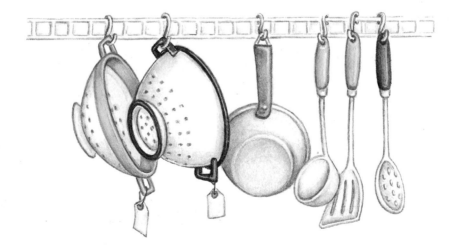

A double batch of Skillet Bowtie Lasagna is a delightful, budget-friendly meal for a casual get-together with friends. Just add warm garlic bread, a big tossed salad and plenty of paper napkins!

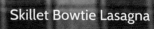
Skillet Bowtie Lasagna

Sunday Meatball Skillet

Sunday Meatball Skillet

*Delicious alongside steamed green beans and a bowl
of homemade applesauce!*

8-oz. pkg. medium egg noodles,
    uncooked
3/4 lb. ground beef
1 c. onion, grated
1/2 c. Italian-flavored dry bread
    crumbs
1 egg, beaten

1/4 c. catsup
1/4 t. pepper
2 c. beef broth
1/4 c. all-purpose flour
1/2 c. sour cream
Garnish: chopped fresh parsley

Cook noodles according to package directions; drain. Meanwhile, in a bowl, combine beef, onion, bread crumbs, egg, catsup and pepper. Mix well and shape into one-inch meatballs; add to a lightly greased large cast-iron skillet. Cook over medium heat, turning occasionally, until browned, about 10 minutes. Remove meatballs to paper towels; drain skillet. In a separate bowl, whisk together beef broth and flour; add to skillet. Cook and stir until thickened, about 5 minutes. Stir in sour cream. Add meatballs and cooked noodles to skillet; toss to coat. Cook and stir over low heat until warmed through, about 5 minutes. Garnish with a sprinkle of parsley. Serves 4.

93

Making lots of meatballs? Grab a mini ice cream scoop or melon baller and start scooping...you'll be done in record time!

Easy Cheesy Ratatouille

*A perfect meatless potluck recipe...they'll go back for seconds,
then ask for the recipe!*

1 eggplant, peeled and cut into
  1-inch cubes
1 zucchini, cut into 1-inch cubes
1 onion, diced
1 red pepper, diced
1/4 c. sun-dried tomato vinaigrette
  salad dressing
14-1/2 oz. can diced tomatoes
1/4 c. grated Parmesan cheese
1 c. shredded mozzarella cheese

In a large cast-iron skillet over medium heat, sauté fresh vegetables with salad dressing until softened. Add tomatoes with juice; cook for 15 minutes. Sprinkle with cheeses. Transfer skillet to oven. Bake, uncovered, at 350 degrees for 15 minutes, or until vegetables are tender. Serves 6 to 8.

Steam veggies to keep their fresh-picked taste. Bring 1/2 inch of water to a boil in a saucepan and add cut-up veggies. Cover and cook for 3 to 5 minutes, to desired tenderness. A quick toss with a little butter and they're ready to enjoy.

Easy Cheesy Ratatouille

Pork Chops Olé

Pork Chops Olé

So easy and so tasty. Make it spicier by adding a little chopped jalapeño.

2 T. oil
4 thick bone-in pork chops
2 T. butter
6.8-oz. pkg. Spanish-flavored rice
  vermicelli mix

14-1/2 oz. can Mexican-style
  stewed tomatoes
1-1/2 c. water
Garnish: sour cream, chopped fresh
  cilantro

Heat oil in a large cast-iron skillet over medium heat. Cook pork chops in oil until browned on both sides, about 6 minutes; remove from skillet and keep warm. Melt butter in same skillet; add rice mix to butter. Cook and stir until rice mix is lightly golden. Stir in tomatoes with juice and water. Return pork chops to skillet and bring to a boil. Reduce heat to low; cover and cook for 20 to 30 minutes, until liquid is absorbed and pork chops are no longer pink in the center. Garnish with sour cream and a sprinkle of cilantro. Makes 4 servings.

Potatoes, Sausage & Peppers

*A delicious one-pot meal...serve with hearty bread
to enjoy every drop of gravy!*

1 T. olive oil
4 Italian pork sausage links
1 green pepper, sliced
1 red pepper, sliced
1-1/3 c. water
1.35-oz. pkg. onion soup mix

3 potatoes, baked, peeled and
  cubed
salt and pepper to taste
Optional: 1/4 c. water,
  2 T. all-purpose flour

Heat oil in a large cast-iron skillet over medium heat; add sausage links and cook until browned. Remove sausages to a plate; cover and set aside, reserving drippings in skillet. Add peppers to skillet; sauté for 5 minutes, or until peppers begin to soften. Stir in water, soup mix and potatoes. Bring to a boil. Cover; simmer for 10 to 15 minutes, until potatoes are heated through and tender. Season with salt and pepper. If a thicker gravy is desired, shake together water and flour in a small jar; add to skillet. Cook and stir over medium-high heat until thickened. Serve potatoes and pan gravy with sausages. Serves 4.

Deep-Dish Skillet Pizza

You'll never go back to take-out pizza after you've sampled this!

1 loaf frozen bread dough, thawed
1 to 2   15-oz. jars pizza sauce
1/2 lb. ground pork sausage,
   browned and drained
5-oz. pkg. sliced pepperoni
1/2 c. sliced mushrooms
1/2 c. green pepper, sliced
Italian seasoning to taste
1 c. shredded mozzarella cheese
1 c. shredded Cheddar cheese

Generously grease a large cast-iron skillet. Press thawed dough into the bottom and up the sides of skillet. Spread desired amount of pizza sauce over dough. Top with remaining ingredients, ending with cheeses. Transfer skillet to oven. Bake, uncovered, at 425 degrees for 30 minutes. Remove from oven. Let stand several minutes; pizza will finish baking in the skillet. Cut into wedges to serve. Serves 4.

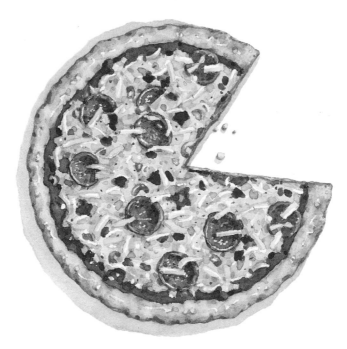

A make-it-yourself pizza party is great for pizza-loving youngsters!
Set out ready-to-bake pizza crusts and lots of toppings and let party
guests be creative.

Deep-Dish Skillet Pizza

Pepperoni Tortellini

Pepperoni Tortellini

Fancy enough for adults, but fun and tasty enough for kids.
Happy eating!

8-oz. pkg. refrigerated 3-cheese
   tortellini pasta, uncooked
2 t. olive oil
1 onion, sliced
1 red pepper, thinly sliced
3 to 4 cloves garlic, chopped
5-oz. pkg. sliced pepperoni, cut
   into strips

1-1/2 t. dried basil
1-1/2 t. dried oregano
1 t. Italian seasoning
1 t. garlic powder
1/2 t. salt
1/4 t. pepper
Garnish: shredded Parmesan
   cheese, fresh basil

Cook pasta according to package directions; drain. Meanwhile, heat oil in a cast-iron skillet over medium heat. Sauté onion, red pepper and garlic until crisp-tender. Add remaining ingredients except pasta and garnish. Cook, stirring occasionally, for 5 minutes. Stir in cooked pasta; simmer until heated through. Garnish with Parmesan cheese and basil. Serves 4 to 6.

Twisty bread sticks are tasty with pasta dishes. Brush refrigerated bread stick dough with a little beaten egg and dust with Italian seasoning, then pop 'em in the oven and bake until toasty.

Too-Much-Zucchini Stovetop Dinner

*A scrumptious hearty dish for when your garden
is overflowing with zucchini!*

3 c. elbow macaroni, uncooked
2 T. olive oil
1 onion, chopped
2 cloves garlic, minced
1 lb. ground beef
1/2 lb. ground Italian pork sausage
3 to 4 zucchini, quartered and
   sliced 1/2-inch thick
14-1/2 oz. can crushed tomatoes

26-oz. jar spaghetti sauce
6-oz. can tomato paste
1/2 c. water
1/2 t. dried basil
1/2 t. dried oregano
1/2 t. garlic powder
salt and pepper to taste
8-oz. pkg. shredded mozzarella
   cheese

Cook macaroni according to package directions; drain. Meanwhile, add oil
to a large cast-iron skillet over medium heat. Sauté onion and garlic until
tender, about 5 minutes. Add beef and sausage; cook until browned. Drain;
stir in zucchini, tomatoes with juice and remaining ingredients except
mozzarella cheese. Cover and simmer for 10 to 15 minutes, until zucchini is
tender. Add seasonings; top with cheese. Serve zucchini mixture ladled over
cooked macaroni. Serves 6 to 8.

Mmm...fresh air always makes us hungry! One-dish skillet suppers are
perfect for a campfire cookout. Save time by chopping the veggies at
home and placing them in small bags for the cooler. Or choose a recipe
with mostly canned ingredients...don't forget the can-opener!

Too-Much-Zucchini Stovetop Dinner

Skillet Chicken with Vegetables & Herbs

Skillet Chicken with Vegetables & Herbs

A complete dinner of roast chicken and veggies...all in one pan!

2 T. all-purpose flour
1/8 t. pepper
1/8 t. paprika
4 chicken breasts
2 T. olive oil
2 red onions, quartered

1 lb. new potatoes, quartered
8-oz. pkg. baby carrots
1-1/2 c. chicken broth
3 T. lemon juice
1 T. fresh oregano, chopped
Garnish: chopped fresh thyme

Combine flour and seasonings in a shallow bowl; coat chicken breasts well. Heat oil in a large cast-iron skillet over medium-high heat. Brown chicken on both sides. Remove chicken from skillet and set aside; reserve drippings in skillet. Add onions and potatoes to skillet; cook for 5 minutes. Add carrots, chicken broth, lemon juice and oregano; bring to a boil. Return chicken to skillet. Cover skillet and transfer to oven. Bake at 350 degrees for 20 minutes. Uncover and bake an additional 15 minutes, or until chicken juices run clear and vegetables are tender. Garnish with a sprinkle of thyme. Serves 4.

Laughter is the best dinnertime music.
-Carleton Kendrick

Cayenne Fried Chicken

Warm up with this hot & spicy version of classic fried chicken. We guarantee you'll come back for seconds!

4 boneless, skinless chicken
   breasts
2-1/2 c. milk
2 T. plus 4 drops hot pepper sauce
1 t. salt
3/4 c. all-purpose flour, divided

2/3 c. butter, divided
6 T. oil
1/2 t. garlic powder
1 t. fresh chives, chopped
salt and pepper to taste

Place chicken in a deep bowl. Cover with milk; add 2 tablespoons hot sauce and salt. Let stand for one hour. Remove chicken and coat with 6 tablespoons flour; set milk mixture aside. In a large cast-iron skillet, heat 1/3 cup butter and oil over medium heat. Add chicken; cook until golden on both sides and no longer pink in the center. Remove chicken to a serving plate; cover to keep warm. Drain skillet, reserving 3 tablespoons drippings in skillet. Add remaining butter and flour; cook and stir until butter is melted and flour is golden. Pour reserved milk mixture into skillet. Add remaining hot sauce and other ingredients; bring to a boil. Cook and stir until slightly thickened, about 10 minutes. Spoon sauce over chicken before serving. Makes 4 servings.

Reheat leftover cooked meat so it's fresh and tasty again! Heat a cast-iron skillet over medium-high heat and add a little oil. Add chops or cutlets and cook until crusted and warmed through. Works great with leftover pizza too!

Cayenne Fried Chicken

Maple Pork Chops

Maple Pork Chops

The sweetness of the maple syrup and saltiness of the soy sauce go together so well, you may want to double this recipe!

1/2 c. maple syrup
3 T. soy sauce
2 cloves garlic, minced

4 thick bone-in pork chops
1 T. oil

In a bowl, whisk together maple syrup, soy sauce and garlic; reserve and refrigerate 1/4 cup of mixture. Add pork chops to remaining mixture in bowl. Cover and refrigerate for at least 15 minutes to overnight, turning pork chops occasionally. Drain, discarding mixture in bowl. Heat oil in a large cast-iron skillet over medium-high heat. Add pork chops. Cook until golden and no longer pink in the center, about 5 minutes per side. At serving time, warm reserved syrup mixture; drizzle over pork chops. Makes 4 servings.

When pork chops are on the menu, sprinkle a little salt in your cast-iron skillet before adding the oil and the meat. You'll have less spattering and more flavorful pork chops.

Creole Pork Chops & Rice

This flavorful one-pot meal really smells amazing as it cooks!
Try it with boneless, skinless chicken breasts too.

1 T. oil
4 thick bone-in pork chops
1 c. onion, diced
1 c. celery, diced

15-oz. can diced tomatoes
1 c. long-cooking rice, uncooked
29-oz. can tomato sauce
salt and pepper to taste

Heat oil in a large cast-iron skillet over medium heat. Add pork chops, onion and celery; cook until pork chops are golden but still pink in the center. Stir in tomatoes with juice, uncooked rice and remaining ingredients. Reduce heat to low. Cover and simmer until rice is tender, about 15 to 20 minutes, adding a little water as needed to prevent drying out. Makes 4 servings.

Skillet BBQ Chicken

A delicious family favorite that uses pantry staples...
great for busy-night suppers!

2 to 3 T. olive oil
4 bone-in or boneless chicken
  breasts
1 onion, sliced
2/3 c. catsup
2/3 c. water
3 T. red wine vinegar

3 T. brown sugar, packed
1 T. Worcestershire sauce
1 t. chili powder
1/2 t. dry mustard
1/2 t. celery seed
Optional: chopped fresh parsley

In a large cast-iron skillet, heat oil over medium-high heat. Brown chicken on both sides; remove to a plate. Add onion to skillet; sauté until tender. Stir in remaining ingredients except garnish; bring to a boil. Return chicken to skillet, skin-side down. Reduce heat to medium-low; cover and cook for 30 minutes. Turn chicken over; cover and simmer an additional 20 minutes, or until chicken juices run clear when pierced. To serve, spoon sauce from skillet over chicken. Garnish with parsley, if desired. Serves 4.

Creole Pork Chops & Rice

Summer Penne Pasta

Skillet Meals & Mains

Summer Penne Pasta

Bored with picnic potato salad? This quick pasta dish
has such a fresh taste.

2 T. olive oil
1 to 2 cloves garlic, pressed
2 c. broccoli flowerets
1 carrot, peeled and cut into thin
   strips

2 c. vegetable broth
8-oz. pkg. penne pasta, uncooked
1/2 t. lemon juice
salt and pepper to taste
1/2 c. grated Parmesan cheese

Heat oil in a deep cast-iron skillet over medium heat. Sauté garlic just until golden. With a slotted spoon, remove garlic from skillet, reserving oil. Add broccoli and carrot to skillet and cook 2 minutes, just until heated through. In a separate saucepan or microwave, bring vegetable broth to a boil; add to skillet. Stir in uncooked pasta and reserved garlic. Cook for 5 minutes, or until pasta is almost tender. Cover; continue cooking over medium heat for 10 minutes, or until pasta and vegetables are tender. Sprinkle in lemon juice, salt and pepper. Toss with Parmesan cheese; serve warm. Serves 4.

Tropical Fish Fillets

A little taste of the tropics...so nice in the middle of winter!

1 lime, halved
4 red snapper or salmon fillets
1 onion, chopped
1 stalk celery, diced
3 cloves garlic, minced

2 T. olive oil
1/2 c. canned coconut milk
1/2 c. salsa
cooked rice

Squeeze lime juice over fish fillets; set aside. In a cast-iron skillet over medium heat, sauté onion, celery and garlic in olive oil until tender. Stir in coconut milk and salsa. Simmer for 10 minutes, stirring occasionally. Add fish, skin-side up, gently pushing it into the sauce. Simmer for 5 to 10 minutes, until fish flakes easily with a fork. Transfer fish to a serving platter; keep warm. Continue to simmer sauce in skillet over low heat until thickened. Ladle some of the sauce over fish; serve any remaining sauce on the side with cooked rice. Serves 4.

Salmon Cornbread Cakes

A different take on traditional salmon croquettes that your family will love. For the cornbread, use leftover cornbread or bake up a small corn muffin mix.

2 T. mayonnaise
2 eggs, beaten
1 t. dried parsley
3 green onions, thinly sliced
1 t. seafood seasoning

1 to 2 t. Worcestershire sauce
14-3/4 oz. can salmon, drained
    and bones removed
2 c. cornbread, crumbled
1 T. canola oil

Combine mayonnaise, eggs, parsley, green onions, seafood seasoning and Worcestershire sauce. Mix well; fold in in salmon and cornbread. Shape into 6 to 8 patties. Heat oil in a cast-iron skillet over medium heat. Cook patties for 3 to 4 minutes on each side, until golden. Serves 6.

Whip up a tasty sauce for salmon or crab cakes...whisk together 1/2 cup sour cream, 1-1/2 tablespoons Dijon mustard, a tablespoon of lemon juice and 2 teaspoons of dill weed. Chill...so simple, so good!

Salmon Cornbread Cakes

Nanny's Famous Beef Stroganoff

Nanny's Famous Beef Stroganoff

Saucy beef and noodles...perfect for Sunday dinner.

1/4 c. butter, divided
1/2 lb. sliced mushrooms
1 onion, chopped
2 lbs. beef round steak, thinly
   sliced and cut into 2-1/2 inch
   strips
1/4 to 1/2 c. all-purpose flour

10-1/2 oz. can beef broth
3/4 c. water
1 t. salt
16-oz. pkg. wide egg noodles,
   uncooked
8-oz. container sour cream

Melt 2 tablespoons butter in a large cast-iron skillet over medium heat; sauté mushrooms and onion. Remove mushroom mixture to a bowl and set aside. Toss beef strips in flour, coating thoroughly. Add remaining butter to skillet and brown beef on all sides. Add beef broth, water and salt; reduce heat to low. Cover and simmer until beef is tender, stirring occasionally, about 1-1/2 hours. While beef mixture is simmering, cook noodles as directed on package; drain. Add mushroom mixture and sour cream to skillet; heat through. Serve over cooked noodles. Serves 6.

Even a simple family supper can be memorable when it's thoughtfully served. Use the good china, set out cloth napkins and a vase of fresh flowers...after all, who's more special than your family?

Chicken & Rotini Stir-Fry

This very tasty, light recipe is so easy to make. You'll love it!

2-1/2 c. rotini pasta, uncooked
2 T. olive oil
2 boneless, skinless chicken
   breasts, cut into strips
1 c. broccoli flowerets
1 c. carrots, peeled and cut into
   curls with a vegetable peeler

1/2 c. red onion, sliced
1/4 c. water
1/2 t. chicken bouillon granules
1/2 t. fresh tarragon, snipped
2 T. grated Parmesan cheese

Cook pasta as directed on package; drain. Meanwhile, heat oil in a large cast-iron skillet over medium-high heat. Add chicken, broccoli, carrots and onion. Cook and stir until broccoli is crisp-tender, about 10 minutes. Add water, bouillon and tarragon; cook and stir until chicken is cooked through. Add pasta and Parmesan cheese. Toss to coat; serve immediately. Makes 4 to 6 servings.

Slice stir-fry meat and veggies into equal-size pieces...they'll all be cooked to perfection at the same time.

Chicken & Rotini Stir-Fry

Grandma's Creole Beef

Grandma's Creole Beef

An old-fashioned recipe that's just as yummy made with ground pork.

2 lbs. ground beef
3/4 c. onion, minced
2 t. garlic, minced
8-oz. can tomato sauce
6-oz. can tomato paste
1/4 c. catsup

1 c. water
2 T. onion powder
16-oz. pkg. elbow macaroni,
   uncooked
salt and pepper to taste

Brown beef in a large cast-iron skillet over medium heat; drain. Add remaining ingredients except macaroni, salt and pepper; stir until well mixed. Cover and simmer over medium-low heat for 30 minutes, stirring occasionally. While sauce is simmering, cook macaroni according to package directions; drain. Place cooked macaroni in a large serving bowl. Pour sauce over macaroni and toss well. Add salt and pepper to taste. Serves 8.

Jensen Family Hash

A simple recipe kids of all ages will love.

2 T. butter
16-oz. pkg. hot dogs, cut into
   bite-size pieces
1 onion, chopped

6 potatoes, cubed
1/4 to 1/2 c. water
salt and pepper to taste
2 to 3 T. catsup

Melt butter in a large cast-iron skillet over medium heat. Add hot dogs and onion; cook until onion is translucent. Stir in potatoes and water; season with salt and pepper. Cover and cook for 10 to 15 minutes, until potatoes are tender. Add catsup; stir well to form a sauce and heat through. Serves 4 to 6.

Pasta Puttanesca

Looking for a new meatless main? This is quick,
inexpensive and magnificent!

8-oz. pkg. spaghetti, uncooked
3 to 6 cloves garlic, chopped
1/8 t. red pepper flakes
1/3 c. olive oil
2 15-oz. cans diced tomatoes,
  drained

1/8 t. dried oregano
3.8-oz. can chopped black olives,
  drained
1/4 c. dried parsley
Garnish: grated Parmesan cheese

Cook spaghetti as directed on package; drain. Meanwhile, in a cast-iron skillet over medium heat, sauté garlic and red pepper flakes in oil until golden. Add tomatoes with juice and oregano. Reduce heat to low and simmer for 20 minutes, stirring occasionally. Stir in olives and parsley; cook for another 2 minutes. Add cooked spaghetti to skillet; toss to mix. Sprinkle with Parmesan cheese. Makes 4 servings.

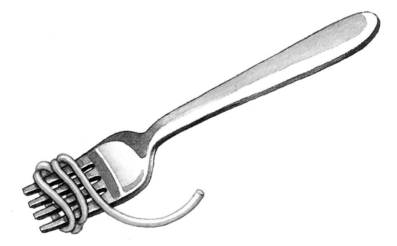

He who enjoys good health is rich, though he knows it not.
-Italian Proverb

Pasta Puttanesca

Tangy Chicken Piccata

Tangy Chicken Piccata

A family favorite that's worthy of a holiday meal! Serve with a savory rice pilaf and a fresh spinach salad.

1 lb. boneless, skinless chicken
   breasts
2 T. all-purpose flour
1 T. oil
1/2 c. orange juice

1/4 c. orange marmalade
1/4 c. honey mustard
1/4 t. dried rosemary
1 orange, peeled, quartered and
   thinly sliced

Dredge chicken in flour; set aside. Heat oil in a large cast-iron skillet over medium heat. Add chicken and cook for 5 minutes, or until golden on both sides. Add orange juice, marmalade, mustard and rosemary; bring to a boil. Reduce heat to low. Simmer for 5 minutes, or until chicken juices run clear. Stir in orange slices and heat through. Serves 4.

Crispy Herbed Chicken Thighs

For the best flavor, use bone-in chicken with the skin on.

6 chicken thighs
salt and pepper to taste
1 T. oil

3 to 4 sprigs fresh thyme, oregano
   or rosemary

Season chicken generously with salt and pepper; set aside. Heat oil in a cast-iron skillet over high heat until hot. Add chicken, skin-side down; cook for 2 minutes. Reduce heat to medium-high. Cook for another 12 minutes, or until golden, occasionally rearranging chicken pieces in skillet but not turning them over. Add herbs around chicken. Transfer skillet to oven. Bake, uncovered, at 475 degrees for 13 to 15 minutes. Turn chicken over; bake another 5 minutes, or until juices run clear. Transfer chicken to a serving platter. Makes 4 to 6 servings.

Picture-Perfect Paella

This classic Spanish dish is amazingly delicious! If you choose not to use seafood, substitute sausage links, browning them along with the chicken.

3 lbs. chicken thighs and/or
   breasts
2 onions, quartered
1 stalk celery, sliced
2 carrots, peeled and sliced
salt and pepper to taste
6 c. water
2 c. long-cooking rice, uncooked
2 cloves garlic, crushed

1/4 c. oil
1 c. frozen baby peas
1/4 c. diced pimentos, drained
1/2 t. dried oregano
1/8 t. saffron or turmeric
1 lb. uncooked large shrimp, peeled
   and cleaned
12 uncooked clams in shells

In a very large deep cast-iron skillet over medium heat, combine chicken, onions, celery, carrots, salt, pepper and water. Bring to a boil. Reduce heat to medium-low. Cover and simmer for one hour. Remove chicken and vegetables to a platter; reserve 6 cups of the broth in a bowl. Dice chicken and set aside, discarding bones. In the same skillet over medium heat, cook and stir rice and garlic in oil until golden. Add reserved chicken, reserved broth, peas, pimentos and herbs. Cover and cook over low heat for 15 minutes. Add shrimp and clams; cover and cook for another 10 minutes, or until shrimp turn pink and clams have opened. Serves 8.

Start a cooking club with friends...a great way to try new recipes!
Decide on dishes ahead of time, then everyone shops for just a part of
the meal. Get together to cook, then enjoy sharing dinner together.

Picture-Perfect Paella

Seafood Linguine with a Kick

Seafood Linguine with a Kick

*Three kinds of seafood make this spicy pasta dish worthy
of a special occasion.*

16-oz. pkg. linguine pasta,
  uncooked
3 T. butter
3 T. extra-virgin olive oil
8 cloves garlic, pressed
2 shallots, thinly sliced
3 T. red pepper flakes, divided
1/2 lb. scallops

1/2 lb. uncooked large shrimp,
  peeled and cleaned
1/2 lb. imitation crabmeat, chopped
2 28-oz. cans petite diced
  tomatoes, drained
3 T. sugar
2 T. fresh basil, thinly sliced

Cook pasta as directed on package; drain. Meanwhile, combine butter
and oil in a large cast-iron skillet over medium heat. Sauté garlic, shallots
and 1-1/2 tablespoons red pepper flakes until tender. Add scallops and
shrimp; cook for 5 to 10 minutes, until shrimp turn pink. Stir in crabmeat
and heat through. Remove seafood to a plate and keep warm. Add tomatoes,
sugar and remaining red pepper flakes to skillet. Bring to a boil, stirring
occasionally; reduce heat and simmer for 15 minutes. Add basil and
seafood to tomato mixture. To serve, spoon over cooked pasta. Serves 8.

Do you have picky eaters in the family? Encourage kids to take a
no-thank-you helping, or just one bite, of foods they think they don't
like. They may be pleasantly surprised!

Sautéed Tilapia with Lemon Butter Sauce

Serve with steamed green beans and baby new potatoes.

1/4 c. all-purpose flour
salt and pepper to taste
1/2 lb. tilapia fillets, thawed if
  frozen

2 T. olive oil
4 T. butter, divided
juice of 1 lemon

Combine flour, salt and pepper in a shallow dish. Dredge fish in flour mixture; set aside. Heat olive oil and 2 tablespoons butter in a cast-iron skillet over medium-high heat. Sauté fish for 3 minutes on each side. Remove fish to a serving plate; drain and wipe out skillet with a paper towel. Over low heat, melt remaining butter in skillet. Add lemon juice; cook and stir for one minute. Return fish to skillet and warm through. To serve, spoon sauce from skillet over fish. Makes 4 servings.

For mild, fresh-tasting fish, place frozen fillets in a shallow dish, cover with milk and let thaw overnight in the fridge.

Sautéed Tilapia with Lemon Butter Sauce

Once heated, cast-iron pans really hold in the heat...
that's what makes them so terrific for cooking! So before
you start, be sure to have several hot pads nearby, or
better yet, thickly padded oven mitts.

When frying chicken or pork chops, or browning
beef for stew, you'll get the best results if the pan isn't
overcrowded. Use an extra large skillet or cook in two
batches.

A ridged cast-iron grill skillet is handy for grilling
burgers or chops on your stovetop whenever it's too cold
or rainy to use the grill outdoors.

Fluffy hot biscuits are a must with any one-pot meal!
Add a personal touch to refrigerated biscuits...brush
with butter, then sprinkle with dried herbs, coarse salt
or sesame seed before baking.

Warm Sides
& Breads

Rosemary-Garlic Skillet Potatoes

Crisp and golden...such a delicious way to enjoy tiny, fresh new potatoes.

2 to 4 T. olive oil
2 T. butter
1-1/2 lbs. new redskin potatoes,
   sliced 1-inch thick

4 to 5 cloves garlic, minced
2-1/2 t. dried rosemary
1/2 t. salt
1/4 t. pepper

Add enough oil to a cast-iron skillet to cover the bottom; add butter. Melt butter over medium heat and stir to mix with oil. Add potatoes and remaining ingredients. Mix well to coat potatoes thoroughly. Cook over medium heat for about 10 minutes, stirring occasionally, until potatoes are lightly golden. Transfer skillet to oven. Bake, uncovered, at 350 degrees for 30 minutes, or until potatoes are tender. Serves 4.

For the crispest, tastiest fried potatoes, start by adding sliced or cubed potatoes to salted ice water. Soak for 5 minutes or so, then drain well and pat dry before adding to the hot oil.

Rosemary-Garlic Skillet Potatoes

Kale & Potato Casserole

Kale & Potato Casserole

*Warm potatoes, wilted greens and Parmesan cheese
make this a hearty side!*

1/4 c. butter, melted
3 potatoes, thinly sliced
10 leaves fresh kale, finely chopped

5 T. grated Parmesan cheese
salt and pepper to taste

Drizzle melted butter over potatoes in a bowl; mix well. In a greased cast-iron skillet, layer 1/3 each of potatoes, kale and Parmesan cheese; season with salt and pepper. Continue layering and seasoning, ending with cheese. Cover skillet and transfer to oven. Bake at 375 degrees for 30 minutes. Uncover; bake for another 15 to 30 minutes, until potatoes are tender. Serves 4 to 6.

Skillet New Potatoes

*You don't even need to peel the potatoes. Try this with tiny Yukon Gold
potatoes as well as baby redskins...yum!*

2 T. butter
2 T. oil
2 lbs. new potatoes

2 to 3 cloves garlic, chopped
salt and pepper to taste

Melt butter with oil in a large skillet over low heat. Add potatoes, cutting any larger potatoes in half. Sprinkle with garlic; season with salt and pepper. Cover and cook over low heat for 40 to 60 minutes, shaking covered pan occasionally, until potatoes are tender and golden. Season with additional salt and pepper, if desired. Serves 4.

Bacon-Florentine Fettuccine

This incredibly tasty and simple pasta dish is so fast to prepare.

16-oz. pkg. fettuccine pasta,
  uncooked
2 10-oz. pkgs. frozen creamed
  spinach
1/2 lb. bacon

1/8 t. garlic powder
1/2 c. plus 2 T. grated Parmesan
  cheese, divided
pepper to taste

Cook pasta as package directs. Drain, reserving 3/4 cup of cooking liquid. Microwave spinach as directed on package; set aside. Meanwhile, cook bacon in a large cast-iron skillet over medium-high heat until crisp. Remove bacon to paper towels; drain skillet. Add crumbled bacon, spinach and garlic powder to skillet over low heat. Slowly drizzle reserved liquid into skillet until sauce reaches desired consistency. Add cooked pasta; mix gently and heat through. Stir in 1/2 cup Parmesan cheese. Season with pepper; top with remaining cheese. Makes 4 servings.

The best kind of friend is the kind you can sit on a porch swing with, never say a word, then walk away feeling like it was the best conversation you've ever had.
-Arnold Glasow

Bacon-Florentine Fettuccine

Hot Bacon Brussels Sprouts

Hot Bacon Brussels Sprouts

Even if your family tells you they don't like Brussels sprouts,
they'll love these...they are awesome!

3 lbs. Brussels sprouts, trimmed
  and quartered
2 T. olive oil
1 t. salt

10 slices bacon, chopped
1/2 c. balsamic vinegar
2 T. brown sugar, packed
1 t. Dijon mustard

In a large bowl, toss Brussels sprouts with olive oil and salt. Place on a rimmed baking sheet lined with aluminum foil. Bake at 400 degrees for 20 minutes, or until tender. Meanwhile, in a large cast-iron skillet over medium heat, cook bacon until crisp. Remove bacon; drain on paper towels. Reserve 1/4 cup drippings in skillet. Add vinegar, brown sugar and mustard to skillet. Cook over medium-high heat, stirring often, for 6 minutes, or until mixture is reduced by half. Drizzle sauce over Brussels sprouts, tossing gently to coat. Sprinkle with crumbled bacon. Serves 10 to 12.

141

Save bacon drippings in a jar in the fridge for adding country-style flavor to other dishes. Stir a couple tablespoons of drippings into recipes like cornbread, fried potatoes, greens or gravy.

Corn Sesame Sauté

A perfect side for grilled chicken or steak. If you're lucky enough to have fresh corn, use the kernels from three ears.

10-oz. pkg. frozen corn
3 T. butter, sliced
3 T. green pepper, chopped
3 T. red pepper, chopped
1 clove garlic, minced

2 T. sesame seed
1/4 t. fresh basil, chopped, or more
    to taste
1/2 t. salt
1/8 t. pepper

Cook corn according to package instructions; drain. Meanwhile, combine remaining ingredients in a cast-iron skillet. Cook over medium heat for 5 minutes, stirring occasionally. Add corn and heat through. Makes 6 servings.

For old-fashioned farmhouse charm, group together an assortment of vintage tin graters on a tabletop or mantel, tuck a tea light under each and enjoy their cozy flickering lights.

Corn Sesame Sauté

Rosemary Peppers & Fusilli

Rosemary Peppers & Fusilli

This colorful, flavorful meatless meal is ready to serve in a jiffy.
If you can't find fusilli pasta, try rotini or cavatappi.

12-oz. pkg. fusilli pasta, uncooked
3 T. olive oil
2 red onions, thinly sliced and
   separated into rings
3 red, orange and/or yellow
   peppers, very thinly sliced

5 to 6 cloves garlic, very thinly
   sliced
3 T. dried rosemary
salt and pepper to taste
Garnish: shredded mozzarella
   cheese

Cook pasta according to package directions; drain. Meanwhile, add oil to
a large cast-iron skillet over medium heat. Add onions; cover and cook over
medium heat for 10 minutes. Stir in peppers, garlic and seasonings. Reduce
heat to low. Cover and simmer, stirring occasionally, for an additional
20 minutes. Serve vegetable mixture over cooked pasta, topped with
mozzarella cheese. Makes 6 servings.

Mix up some zesty oil & vinegar salad dressing for dinner tonight.
Combine 3/4 cup olive oil, 1/4 cup white wine vinegar, 3/4 teaspoon
salt and 1/4 teaspoon pepper in a small jar. Add some minced garlic,
if you like. Screw on the lid and shake well. Keep refrigerated.

Hawaiian Asparagus

A delicious new way to enjoy fresh asparagus in season.

1 lb. asparagus, trimmed and cut in
   1-inch diagonal slices
2 T. olive oil
1/4 c. beef broth

4 to 5 slices bacon, crisply cooked
   and crumbled
pepper to taste
2 T. toasted sesame seed

In a cast-iron skillet over medium heat, cook asparagus in oil for 2 to
3 minutes. Add beef broth; reduce heat to low. Cover and simmer for 4 to
5 minutes, until asparagus is cooked to desired tenderness. Stir in crumbled
bacon, pepper and sesame seed. Serves 4

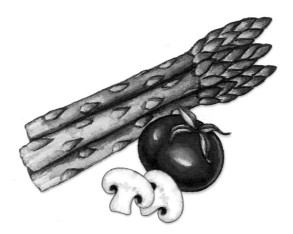

Serve up a Southern-style vegetable plate for dinner. With two or three
scrumptious veggie dishes and a basket of buttery cornbread, no one
will even miss the meat.

Hawaiian Asparagus

Roasted Tomato-Feta Broccoli

Roasted Tomato-Feta Broccoli

*This is such a simple and fast side dish...but don't be fooled,
it's full of flavor!*

2 T. olive oil
2 c. fresh broccoli, cut into
   flowerets
1 c. cherry tomatoes
1 t. lemon juice

dried parsley, salt and pepper to
   taste
1/2 c. crumbled feta cheese
Optional: additional olive oil

Heat olive oil in a cast-iron skillet over medium heat. Add broccoli,
tomatoes, lemon juice and seasonings; cook until vegetables are crisp-
tender. Transfer warm vegetable mixture to a large bowl and mix in cheese.
Drizzle with additional oil, if desired. Serves 3 to 4.

Heat limes or lemons in the microwave for 30 seconds before
squeezing...you'll get twice the juice!

Company Green Beans

A simple way to jazz up green beans.

3 slices bacon
1/4 c. red onion, finely grated
2 t. garlic, minced
2   14-1/2 oz. cans French-style
   green beans, drained

1 tomato, chopped
salt and pepper to taste
1/2 c. shredded sharp Cheddar
   cheese

Cook bacon in a cast-iron skillet over medium-high heat until crisp. Remove bacon to paper towels, reserving drippings in skillet. Sauté onion and garlic in reserved drippings until slightly softened. Remove from heat; stir in green beans, tomato and seasonings. Sprinkle with cheese. Cover skillet and transfer to oven. Bake at 400 degrees for 15 minutes. Uncover; reduce heat to 350 degrees. Bake an additional 15 minutes, until hot and bubbly. Serves 4.

150

Help potluck hosts keep track of dishes by taping a label to the bottom of your dish...be sure to use a waterproof marker and include your name and phone number.

Company Green Beans

Bowties & Blush

Bowties & Blush

A restaurant-style meal in the comfort of your own home...
just add a basket of warm garlic bread.

16-oz. pkg. bowtie pasta,
   uncooked
1 T. butter
1 onion, chopped
1 banana pepper, chopped
2 cloves garlic, chopped
1 T. all-purpose flour

3/4 c. milk
1/2 c. whipping cream
1/2 t. salt
1-1/4 c. spaghetti sauce
1/4 c. grated Parmesan cheese
1/4 c. fresh basil, chopped

Cook pasta according to package directions; drain. Meanwhile, melt butter in a cast-iron skillet over medium heat. Add onion, pepper and garlic; sauté until tender. Stir in flour. Gradually stir in milk, cream and salt; bring to a boil. Stir in spaghetti sauce. Reduce heat to low and simmer for 10 minutes. Remove from heat; pour into a serving bowl. Add cooked pasta; mix gently. Sprinkle with Parmesan cheese and basil just before serving. Serves 8.

153

Aged Parmesan cheese is most flavorful when it's freshly grated.
A chunk of Parmesan will stay fresh in the fridge for several weeks if
wrapped in a paper towel dampened with cider vinegar and then
tucked into a plastic zipping bag.

Meggie's Ratatouille

Taking this veggie-packed dish to a potluck? Be sure to have copies of the recipe handy...you're sure to be asked!

1 eggplant, peeled and cut into
  1-inch cubes
1 onion, diced
1 red pepper, diced
1 zucchini, cut into 1-inch cubes

1/4 c. sun-dried tomato salad
  dressing
14-1/2 oz. can diced tomatoes
1/4 c. grated Parmesan cheese
1 c. shredded mozzarella cheese

Combine fresh vegetables and salad dressing in a large cast-iron skillet. Sauté over medium heat until vegetables are softened. Add tomatoes with juice. Reduce heat to low and simmer for 15 minutes, stirring occasionally. Sprinkle with cheeses. Transfer skillet to oven. Bake, uncovered, at 350 degrees for 15 minutes, or until bubbly and cheeses are melted. Serves 6 to 8.

After groceries are unpacked, take just a little time to chop fruits and vegetables and place them in plastic zipping bags. Weeknight dinners will be so much easier!

Meggie's Ratatouille

Skillet Squash Succotash

Skillet Squash Succotash

Need a new way to serve all that summer squash from the garden? Try this!

1 T. butter
1 T. oil
4 yellow squash, thinly sliced
10-oz. can diced tomatoes with
  green chiles

11-oz. can corn, drained
1 t. garlic powder

Melt butter with oil in a cast-iron skillet over medium heat. Add squash and cook until golden, stirring occasionally. Stir in remaining ingredients. Reduce heat; cover and simmer for 20 minutes. Makes 4 to 6 servings.

Plant a veggie garden! Even a single potted tomato plant on the patio can produce lots of ripe, juicy tomatoes. If you're new to gardening, get free advice from the local garden store or library.

Basil-Broccoli Pasta

Serve this dish as either a yummy side or a meatless main.

16-oz. pkg. rigatoni pasta,
   uncooked
6 T. olive oil
2 T. butter
4 cloves garlic, sliced
1 bunch broccoli, sliced into
   flowerets

1 c. vegetable broth
pepper to taste
Garnish: chopped fresh basil,
   grated Parmesan cheese

Cook pasta according to package directions; drain. Meanwhile, melt butter with oil in a large deep cast-iron skillet over medium heat. Add garlic; cook until lightly golden. Add broccoli; increase heat to medium-high. Cook, stirring often, until broccoli is almost tender, about 3 to 4 minutes. Pour in vegetable broth; reduce heat to low. Cover and simmer until broccoli is tender. Stir cooked pasta into mixture in skillet; mix thoroughly and heat through. Season with pepper. Top with basil and Parmesan cheese. Serves 4 to 6.

Don't toss out the stalks when preparing fresh broccoli...they're good to eat too! Peel stalks with a potato peeler, then chop or dice and add to salads and soups.

Basil-Broccoli Pasta

Saucy Limas

Saucy Limas

These are some of the best lima beans you'll ever taste! They've got a tangy kick that will have you coming back for more.

2 10-oz. pkgs. frozen baby lima
  beans
1/2 c. catsup
1/4 c. molasses

1 T. mustard
1 T. vinegar
1/8 t. Worcestershire sauce
1/8 t. hot pepper sauce

Cook lima beans in a cast-iron skillet according to package directions. Drain; stir in remaining ingredients. Simmer over medium-low heat for 5 to 10 minutes, stirring occasionally, until heated through. Serves 6.

Take the kids along whenever you visit a farmstand. Let each child choose a vegetable and let them help prepare it. Even picky eaters will be more likely to eat their very own veggies!

Grandma's Skillet Tomatoes

This recipe is so easy and it's always a hit with the guys!

1/4 c. milk
1/2 c. seasoned dry bread crumbs
1 T. green onion, minced
1 T. grated Parmesan cheese
1 t. Italian seasoning

1 t. salt
6 ripe tomatoes, sliced 1/2-inch
   thick
1/4 c. olive oil, divided
1/2 c. shredded mozzarella cheese

Place milk in a shallow bowl. In a separate bowl, combine bread crumbs, green onion, Parmesan cheese and seasonings; mix well. Dip tomatoes into milk; coat with crumb mixture. Heat 2 tablespoons oil in a cast-iron skillet over medium-high heat. Cook tomatoes, a few at a time, until golden, about 2 minutes per side. Add more oil, as needed. Remove tomatoes to a serving plate; sprinkle with mozzarella cheese. Serves 6.

162

At the first sign of frost, pick your tomatoes, wrap each individually in newspaper and store in a loosely covered box in a cool, dark spot. They'll ripen slowly and keep for weeks.

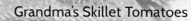
Grandma's Skillet Tomatoes

Saucy Zucchini & Tomatoes

Warm Sides & Breads

Saucy Zucchini & Tomatoes

*Serve with crusty bread and a tall glass of icy sweet tea
for a delightfully simple lunch.*

2 T. bacon drippings or olive oil
1 onion, sliced
1 c. tomatoes, chopped

1/2 bay leaf
salt and pepper to taste
3 zucchini, sliced 1-inch thick

Heat drippings or olive oil in a cast-iron skillet over medium heat. Add onion; sauté until translucent. Add tomatoes, bay leaf, salt and pepper; simmer for 5 minutes. Add zucchini; cover and simmer until tender, about 8 to 10 minutes. Discard bay leaf before serving. Serves 4 to 6.

Garlicky Skillet-Roasted Broccoli

So much more flavorful than plain old steamed broccoli!

1 T. olive oil
2 cloves garlic, thinly sliced
1 bunch broccoli, cut into flowerets

1/4 t. red pepper flakes
salt and pepper to taste
3 T. water

Heat oil in a cast-iron skillet over medium-low heat. Add garlic; cook and stir for about one minute, just until golden but not browned. With a slotted spoon, remove garlic to a small bowl, reserving drippings in skillet. Increase heat to medium-high. Add broccoli and seasonings; drizzle with water. Cover and cook for about 3 minutes. Uncover; cook and stir until broccoli is crisp-tender and lightly golden. Sprinkle with reserved garlic before serving. Makes 4 servings.

Texas Hominy

Great for cookouts...serve right from the skillet!
Feel free to mix yellow and white hominy.

6 slices bacon, diced
1 onion, finely diced
1 jalapeño pepper, minced and
   seeds removed
2 cloves garlic, minced
4 15-1/2 oz. cans hominy, drained

salt and pepper to taste
1-1/2 c. shredded Cheddar cheese,
   divided
1-1/2 c. shredded Monterey Jack
   cheese, divided
1/2 c. green onion tops, chopped

Cook bacon in a large cast-iron skillet over medium heat until crisp.
Remove bacon to paper towels; reserve drippings in skillet. Sauté onion
and jalapeño pepper in reserved drippings until tender. Add garlic; cook one
to 2 minutes longer. Stir in hominy, salt and pepper. Remove from heat. Stir
in one cup each of Cheddar and Monterey Jack cheeses. Smooth out mixture
evenly in skillet. Top with remaining cheeses, crumbled bacon and green
onions. Transfer skillet to oven. Bake, uncovered, at 375 degrees for
30 minutes, until hot and bubbly. Makes 10 servings.

166

Have a chuckwagon-style cookout! Alongside burgers on the grill, serve
up Texas Hominy, with the cast-iron skillet set right on the grill. Add a
side of cornbread and keep bandannas on hand for fun
lap-size napkins.

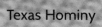
Texas Hominy

Gran's Mushrooms in Sour Cream

Gran's Mushrooms in Sour Cream

A scrumptious recipe to serve with your favorite grilled steak or baked chicken.

1 onion, chopped
2 T. butter
16-oz. pkg. sliced mushrooms
8-oz. container sour cream

1 t. dill weed
1/2 t. garlic powder
salt and pepper to taste
Optional: 1 T. all-purpose flour

In a cast-iron skillet over medium heat, sauté onion in butter until translucent. Add mushrooms; cook until soft and lightly golden. Stir in sour cream and seasonings. If mixture is thinner than desired, stir in flour. Cover and cook over low heat until heated through. Makes 4 to 6 servings.

Having a roast for dinner? Whip up some delicious pan gravy! Place the roast on a platter and pour the pan juices into a skillet. Whisk together 1/4 cup cold water and 1/4 cup cornstarch and add to the skillet. Cook and stir over medium heat until gravy comes to a boil and thickens, 5 to 10 minutes. Season with salt and pepper.

Savory Rice Casserole

*A delicious and super easy side dish...it can bake
alongside chicken or pork chops.*

8-oz. can sliced water chestnuts,
    drained and liquid reserved
4-oz. can sliced mushrooms,
    drained and liquid reserved

1/2 c. butter, sliced
1 c. long-cooking rice, uncooked
10-1/2 oz. can French onion soup

In a cast-iron skillet over medium heat, sauté water chestnuts and
mushrooms in butter. Add uncooked rice, soup and reserved liquids. Cover
skillet tightly; transfer to oven. Bake at 375 degrees for 45 to 60 minutes,
until rice is tender. Serves 6 to 8.

Roasted or grilled vegetables are delicious warm or cold! Slice zucchini,
cauliflower, sweet peppers, mushrooms or asparagus. Toss with olive
oil and spread in a cast-iron skillet. Bake at 350 degrees, stirring
occasionally, for about 30 minutes, until tender.

Savory Rice Casserole

Hoppin' Jane

Hoppin' Jane

*A quick & easy take on Hoppin' John, a traditional
New Year's Day favorite.*

4 slices bacon, coarsely chopped
1/2 c. onion, chopped
1/4 c. celery, chopped
1/4 c. red pepper, chopped
2 cloves garlic, pressed
1-1/4 c. instant rice, uncooked

16-oz. can black-eyed peas,
   drained
1 c. water
1 c. chicken broth
salt and pepper to taste

In a cast-iron skillet over medium-high heat, cook bacon until crisp. With
a slotted spoon, remove bacon to paper towels. Reserve 2 teaspoons
drippings in skillet. Add onion, celery, red pepper and garlic to drippings;
sauté for 3 minutes, or until softened. Stir in uncooked rice and remaining
ingredients. Bring to a boil over high heat. Cover; remove from heat and let
stand 5 minutes, or until rice is tender. Stir again before serving; garnish
with crisp bacon. Serves 4.

Sweet-and-Sour Green Beans

*If you like tangy sweet-and-sour flavors, this cool side dish
will be a new favorite.*

6 slices bacon
2/3 c. white vinegar
1/3 c. water
2/3 c. sugar

2 14-1/2 oz. cans green beans,
   drained
1/2 onion, sliced

In a cast-iron skillet over medium-high heat, cook bacon until crisp.
Remove bacon to paper towels; reserve 2 tablespoons drippings in skillet.
Add vinegar and water to skillet; bring to a boil. Slowly add sugar, stirring
until dissolved. Add green beans and stir. Place onion slices on top of
beans. Let boil for about 2 minutes; remove from heat. Transfer bean
mixture to a serving bowl. Cover and refrigerate for about 2 hours, stirring
occasionally. At serving time, top with crumbled bacon. Makes 6 servings.

Honeyed Carrots

Honeyed Carrots

The sweet taste of these carrots makes this a very popular dish!

5 c. carrots, peeled and sliced
1/4 c. honey
1/4 c. butter, melted
2 T. brown sugar, packed

2 T. fresh parsley, chopped
1/4 t. salt
1/8 t. pepper

Place carrots in a cast-iron skillet; add water to cover. Cook over medium heat just until tender; drain and return to skillet. Combine remaining ingredients in a small bowl and blend well. Pour honey mixture over carrots; toss to coat. Cook over medium heat until carrots are glazed and heated through. Makes 8 servings.

Mack's Honey Apple Rings

A scrumptious garnish for baked pork chops or grilled sausage links.

1/2 c. honey
2 T. vinegar
1/4 t. cinnamon

1/4 t. salt
4 Golden Delicious apples, cored
and cut into 1/2-inch rings

175

Combine honey, vinegar and seasonings in a cast-iron skillet; bring to a boil over medium heat. Add apple rings to skillet. Reduce heat to medium-low. Simmer for 8 to 10 minutes until tender, turning apples once. Makes 4 servings.

Sour Cream Cornbread

This flavorful cornbread is a must with ham & beans, chili and so many other comfort foods.

1-1/2 c. self-rising cornmeal
2 T. self-rising flour
1/4 c. sugar
2 eggs, beaten

1-1/2 c. sour cream
2/3 c. oil
1/2 c. buttermilk

Combine all ingredients in a large bowl and mix well. Pour batter into a greased cast-iron skillet. Transfer skillet to oven. Bake, uncovered, at 350 degrees for 25 to 30 minutes, until golden. Cut into wedges or squares; serve warm. Makes 8 servings.

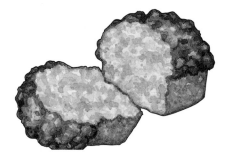

Mississippi Hushpuppies

Irresistible little morsels! Try them with mustard for dipping.

3/4 c. self-rising cornmeal
1/2 c. self-rising flour
1-1/2 T. baking powder
3 eggs, beaten

1/2 c. onion, diced
1/4 c. buttermilk
oil for deep frying

In a bowl, combine cornmeal, flour, baking powder, eggs and onion. Stir in enough buttermilk to moisten mixture; stir until well mixed. Heat several inches of oil in a cast-iron skillet over medium-high heat. Working in batches, drop batter into hot oil by teaspoonfuls. Fry until golden on both sides. Drain on paper towels; serve warm. Makes 2 dozen.

Sour Cream Cornbread

Sesame Skillet Bread

Sesame Skillet Bread

Stir up a panful of warm bread for tonight's dinner in a snap!

1-1/3 c. cornmeal
2/3 c. whole-wheat flour
2 t. baking powder
1 t. salt
1/4 c. wheat germ

2 T. sesame seed
1 3/4 c. milk
3 T. oil
1 egg, beaten

In a bowl, stir together cornmeal, flour, baking powder, salt, wheat germ and sesame seed. Add milk, oil and egg; stir until moistened. Spoon batter into a greased cast-iron skillet; transfer to oven. Bake, uncovered, at 400 degrees for 25 to 30 minutes. Cut into wedges; serve warm. Serves 8.

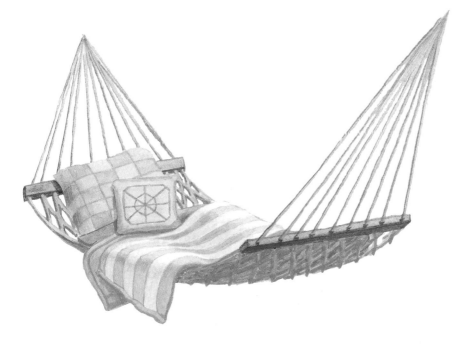

Pair up a cast-iron skillet and the ingredients for Sesame Skillet Bread for a cook on your gift list. Wrap it all up in a cheery red bandanna. Be sure to tie on a recipe card!

Whole-Wheat Soda Bread

*A wonderful hearty, coarse-textured bread
that's terrific with soups and stews.*

1 c. all-purpose flour
1 t. baking powder
1 t. baking soda
1/2 t. salt

2 T. sugar
2 c. whole-wheat flour
1-1/2 c. buttermilk
1 T. butter, melted

In a large bowl, combine all-purpose flour, baking powder, baking soda, salt and sugar. Add whole-wheat flour; mix well. Add buttermilk; stir just until moistened. Turn dough onto a floured surface. Knead gently for about 2 minutes, until well mixed and dough is smooth. Form dough into a ball; pat into a circle and place in a lightly greased cast-iron skillet. With a floured knife, mark dough into 4 wedges by cutting halfway through to the bottom. Transfer skillet to oven. Bake, uncovered, at 375 degrees for 30 to 40 minutes, until loaf sounds hollow when tapped. Brush with butter; cool on a wire rack. Serves 4.

Fresh-baked, cooled bread freezes beautifully. Wrap it in plastic, then aluminum foil and freeze for up to 3 weeks.

Whole-Wheat Soda Bread

Minted peas are a fast and fresh side. Place a small package of frozen baby peas in a skillet over medium heat. Cook and stir until peas are just cooked through. Add one tablespoon butter, 1/2 teaspoon sugar, 2 teaspoons snipped fresh mint and a few drops of lemon juice. Toss until mixed well and serve hot.

Make a sink scrubbie by repurposing a plastic mesh bag that held onions or apples...perfect for gently cleaning cast iron. Simply fold the bag several times into a loose bundle and tie with kitchen twine.

A handy all-purpose seasoning to keep by the stove... mix 6 tablespoons salt and one tablespoon pepper and fill a large shaker. It's just right for sprinkling on pork chops, burgers, chicken and homestyle potatoes!

Cast-iron skillets are terrific for cooking, but not so great for food storage...food may pick up metallic tastes from the pan. Instead, remove any leftovers to a glass or plastic container before refrigerating.

Hot & Bubbly Desserts

Hot & Bubbly Desserts

Skillet Cherry Pie

Pop this fast-to-fix pie in the oven...enjoy warm cherry pie after dinner!

1/4 c. butter
1/2 c. brown sugar, packed
2 9-inch frozen pie crusts,
   unbaked
15-oz. can tart cherries, drained

21-oz. can cherry pie filling
1/4 c. sugar
1 T. plus 1/8 t. all-purpose flour
1 to 2 T. milk
Garnish: powdered sugar

In a cast-iron skillet, melt butter with brown sugar over medium-low heat, stirring often. Remove from heat. Place one frozen pie crust in skillet on top of butter mixture; set aside. In a bowl, mix cherries and pie filling; spoon into crust. Mix sugar and flour together in a cup; sprinkle evenly over cherry mixture. Place remaining frozen pie crust upside-down on top of cherry mixture. Brush with milk; cut slits in crust to vent. Transfer skillet to oven. Bake, uncovered, at 350 degrees for one hour, or until bubbly and crust is golden. Cool; sprinkle with powdered sugar. Serves 8.

Slow-Simmered Stone Fruit

Such a practical way of using beautiful summer fruit...it doesn't even matter if it's slightly blemished. Delicious!

2 lbs. peaches, plums, nectarines
   or apricots
4-inch cinnamon stick

1/2 c. orange or apple juice
Garnish: Greek yogurt or whipping
   cream

Cut fruit in half and remove pits; do not peel. Arrange fruit skin-side down in a single layer in a buttered large cast-iron skillet. It's fine to have a few pieces of fruit in a second layer. Push cinnamon stick into fruit. Add fruit juice; more juice will be created as fruit cooks. Transfer skillet to oven. Bake, uncovered, at 350 degrees for 30 to 40 minutes, until fruit is soft and bubbly. Discard cinnamon stick. Serve warm, topped with yogurt or cream. Serves 4 to 6.

Skillet Cherry Pie

Crunchy Oat & Fruit Crisp

Crunchy Oat & Fruit Crisp

A crunchy, fruit-filled crisp that's tasty warm or cold.

1 c. quick-cooking oats, uncooked
3/4 c. brown sugar, packed and
   divided
5 T. all-purpose flour, divided
1/3 c. butter, melted
1 c. blueberries

1 c. cherries, pitted
4 apples, peeled, cored and thickly
   sliced
1/4 c. frozen orange juice
   concentrate, thawed
1 T. cinnamon

In a bowl, combine oats, 1/2 cup brown sugar, 2 tablespoons flour
and butter. Mix until crumbly and set aside. In a separate bowl, combine
fruit, remaining brown sugar and other ingredients. Stir until fruit is
evenly coated. Spoon fruit mixture into a lightly buttered cast-iron skillet;
sprinkle oat mixture over top. Transfer skillet to oven. Bake, uncovered,
at 350 degrees for 30 to 35 minutes, until apples are tender and topping
is golden. Serves 4 to 6.

Bake a fruit crisp outdoors on the grill! Assemble ingredients in a cast-
iron skillet. Preheat grill to medium-low and set skillet in the center.
Grill, covered, for 15 to 20 minutes, until topping is golden and fruit
filling is hot and bubbly. Yum!

Louisiana Pear Cake

Try green Anjou or red Bartlett for this delicious old-fashioned cake.

1/2 c. butter, softened
1 c. sugar
1 egg
1-1/2 c. all-purpose flour
1 T. baking soda
1/4 t. salt

1/2 t. cinnamon
1 t. vanilla extract
2 c. pears, peeled, cored and grated
1/2 c. chopped pecans
Garnish: whipped cream

In a bowl, beat together butter, sugar and egg. In a separate bowl, sift together flour, baking soda, salt and cinnamon; add to sugar mixture. Add vanilla, pears and nuts; mix well. Pour batter into a greased and floured cast-iron skillet. Transfer skillet to oven. Bake, uncovered, at 300 degrees for one hour. Cut into wedges; serve with whipped cream. Makes 8 servings.

188

For quick release when baking a cake in a skillet, line the bottom of the skillet with a circle of parchment paper that's been lightly greased and dusted with flour.

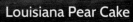
Louisiana Pear Cake

Simple Skillet Peaches

Hot & Bubbly Desserts

Simple Skillet Peaches

These peaches are delicious on just about anything you can think of...hot oatmeal, ice cream or best of all, big slices of angel food cake!

6 c. peaches, peeled, pitted and cut   1/2 c. sugar
   into bite-size pieces   1 T. vanilla extract

Combine peaches and sugar in a large cast-iron skillet over medium heat. Bring to a boil; reduce heat to medium-low. Simmer until peaches are soft and mixture has thickened, about 20 to 25 minutes. Stir in extract. Serve warm, or remove to a covered container and refrigerate. Makes 6 servings.

Any homemade dessert is extra special topped with dollops of whipped cream. It's oh-so simple too. In a chilled bowl, with chilled beaters, whip one cup of whipping cream on high speed until soft peaks form. Mix in 2 teaspoons sugar and 2 teaspoons vanilla extract...and enjoy!

Bananas Foster

A New Orleans treat that can't be beat! It deserves to be served with very best vanilla bean ice cream.

1/4 c. butter, sliced
2/3 c. dark brown sugar, packed
1-1/2 t. vanilla extract
1/2 t. cinnamon
3 T. rum, or 2 t. water plus 1 t. rum
   extract

3 firm bananas, halved lengthwise
   and crosswise
Garnish: vanilla ice cream

Melt butter in a large deep cast-iron skillet over medium heat. Stir in sugar, vanilla, cinnamon and rum or water and extract. Cook and stir until bubbly and sugar is dissolved. Add bananas and cook for one to 2 minutes, until bananas are heated through. To serve, immediately spoon hot mixture over scoops of ice cream. Serves 4.

Freeze leftover ripe bananas for up to 3 months, peel and all! Simply tuck them into plastic freezer bags and pop in the freezer. When it's time to make banana bread, thaw bananas before removing peels.

Bananas Foster

Giant Chocolate Chip Cookie

Giant Chocolate Chip Cookie

What could be better than a huge chocolatey cookie to share with friends?

2 c. all-purpose flour
1 t. baking soda
1/2 t. salt
3/4 c. butter, softened
3/4 c. light brown sugar, packed
1/2 c. sugar

1 egg, beaten
2 t. vanilla extract
3/4 c. semi-sweet chocolate chips
3/4 c. milk chocolate chips
Optional: vanilla ice cream

In a bowl, whisk together flour, baking soda and salt; set aside. In a separate large bowl, stir butter and sugars until light and fluffy. Add egg and vanilla; mix well. Add flour mixture to butter mixture; beat just until blended. Stir in chocolate chips. Transfer dough to a lightly greased cast-iron skillet; gently flatten dough. Transfer skillet to oven. Bake, uncovered, at 350 degrees for 40 to 45 minutes, until golden on top and edges. Do not overbake. Cool cookie in skillet on a wire rack for 15 to 20 minutes; cut into 8 wedges. Serve warm; top each wedge with a scoop of ice cream, if desired. Makes 8 servings.

No-Bake Skillet Cookies

The taste of these little gems is out of this world!

1/2 c. butter, softened
2 c. sugar
1/2 c. baking cocoa
1/2 c. milk
2 c. corn flake cereal

1/2 c. creamy peanut butter
1 t. vanilla extract
1/2 c. semi-sweet chocolate chips
1/2 c. black walnuts, chopped
1/2 c. sweetened flaked coconut

In a large cast-iron skillet over medium heat, combine butter, sugar, cocoa and milk. Bring to a boil; cook for 2 minutes. Remove from heat. Add remaining ingredients; stir to combine. Drop by teaspoonfuls onto wax paper. Let stand for 2 to 3 hours, until set. Makes 3 dozen.

Iron Skillet Apple Pie

Grandma's baking secret...for the most delicious flavor, use a mix of apples like Granny Smith, Gala and Braeburn.

1/2 c. butter
1 c. light brown sugar, packed
2 9-inch pie crusts
4 to 6 cooking apples, peeled, cored
   and sliced

1 c. sugar
2 t. cinnamon
Garnish: vanilla ice cream

Place butter in a cast-iron skillet; place skillet in a 350-degree oven until butter melts. Stir brown sugar into melted butter. Return skillet to oven for 3 to 4 minutes. Place one pie crust over butter mixture in skillet; set aside. Arrange apple slices to fill crust. Mix together sugar and cinnamon; sprinkle over apples. Place second pie crust on top; crimp edges to seal. Make 4 to 6 small slits in crust with a knife tip. Transfer skillet to oven. Bake, uncovered, at 350 degrees for 45 minutes, or until bubbly and crust is lightly golden. Serve warm, topped with ice cream. Makes 6 to 8 servings.

Create a heavenly glaze for any apple dessert. Melt together 1/2 cup butterscotch chips, 2 tablespoons butter and 2 tablespoons whipping cream over low heat.

Iron Skillet Apple Pie

Pineapple Upside-Down Cake

Pineapple Upside-Down Cake

*Keep a pitcher of icy milk on hand. It's a perfect pairing
with this handed-down recipe.*

1/3 c. butter	2 eggs
1/2 c. brown sugar, packed	2/3 c. sugar
20-oz. can pineapple rings, drained	1 t. vanilla extract
and 6 T. juice reserved	1 c. all-purpose flour
8 to 10 maraschino cherries	1 t. baking powder
15 to 20 pecan halves	1/4 t. salt

Melt butter over low heat in a cast-iron skillet; sprinkle brown sugar evenly
over butter. Arrange pineapple rings in skillet. Place a cherry in the center of
each ring; arrange pecan halves around rings and set aside. With an electric
mixer on high speed, beat eggs in a medium bowl until thick and lemon-
colored, about 5 minutes. Gradually beat in sugar; stir in reserved pineapple
juice and vanilla. Add flour, baking powder and salt; mix well. Pour batter
over pineapple rings in skillet. Transfer skillet to oven. Bake, uncovered, at
350 degrees for 30 to 35 minutes. Let cool in skillet for 30 minutes. Invert
skillet on a serving plate; let stand for a minute, then turn cake out of
skillet. Makes 10 to 12 servings.

199

Make Pineapple Upside-Down Cake even more luscious with fresh
pineapple! Cut off the pineapple's top and bottom, stand it upright
and slice off the peel all around with a serrated knife. Then slice the
pineapple crosswise and trim out the core with a paring knife
to form rings.

Apricot & Peach Fried Pies

Just like Great-Granny used to make! Short on time? Substitute refrigerated pie crusts for the homemade dough.

8-oz. pkg. dried apricots, coarsely
  chopped
6-oz. pkg. dried peaches, coarsely
  chopped

3/4 c. sugar
shortening or peanut oil for deep
  frying
Optional: powdered sugar

Combine apricots and peaches in a large saucepan over low heat. Cover with water; stir in sugar. Cover and cook over low heat, stirring occasionally, until fruit is very tender. Uncover; continue to cook until water is evaporated. Meanwhile, prepare Dough; roll out thinly on a lightly floured surface. With a knife, cut around a 6-inch saucer to make 18 circles. Spoon fruit filling evenly onto each dough circle. Fold circles in half; moisten edges with water and seal with a fork. Heat 2 inches of shortening or oil in a deep cast-iron skillet over medium-high heat. Carefully add pies, a few at a time; cook until golden on both sides. Drain on paper towels. Sprinkle with powdered sugar, if desired. Makes 1-1/2 dozen.

Dough:

4 c. all-purpose flour
2 t. salt

1 c. shortening
1 c. milk

Mix together flour and salt. Cut in shortening with 2 knives until mixture is crumbly. Add milk; stir until a dough forms.

Keep a pair of kitchen shears handy...they make quick work of cutting up sticky dried fruit.

Apricot & Peach Fried Pies

Apple Hand Pies

Hot & Bubbly Desserts

Apple Hand Pies

*Can't wait 'til the county fair rolls around again? Whip up
a batch of these yummy pies!*

2 Granny Smith apples, peeled,
  cored and diced
1/3 c. sugar
1/2 t. cinnamon
2 c. all-purpose flour

1 t. salt
1/2 c. shortening
1/2 c. cold water
1 c. peanut oil
Garnish: coarse sugar

Mix apples, sugar and cinnamon in a saucepan over low heat. Cook for 8 to
10 minutes, until apples are tender. Set aside. Combine flour and salt; cut in
shortening with a fork. Stir in water to a dough consistency. Roll out dough
1/8-inch thick on a floured surface. Cut out with a 4-inch round cookie
cutter; place one tablespoon apple mixture in center of each circle. Sprinkle
edges with water; fold circles in half. Seal edges with a fork; set aside. Heat
peanut oil in a cast-iron skillet over medium-high heat. Fry pies, a few at a
time, for 2 to 3 minutes per side, until golden. Drain on paper towels;
sprinkle with coarse sugar while still warm. Makes 6 to 8 servings.

Make Apple Hand Pies really special when taking them to a social.
Wrap each one in wax paper and seal with a pretty label to identify
what's inside.

Prize-Winning Funnel Cakes

The kid in all of us loves the powdered sugar topping! Or treat yourself to a big dollop of fruit pie filling.

2 c. all-purpose flour
1 T. sugar
1 t. baking powder
1/4 t. salt
2 eggs, beaten

1-1/4 c. milk
oil for deep frying
Garnish: powdered sugar
Optional: apple, cherry or blueberry
    pie filling

Sift together flour, sugar, baking powder and salt into a deep bowl. Make a well in the center; add eggs and enough milk to make a thin batter. Mix well. In a cast-iron skillet, heat 2 inches oil to 375 degrees. With a fingertip over end of funnel, drop batter by 1/2 cupfuls into a funnel over hot oil, one at a time, swirling funnel as batter is released. Cook until golden, about 2 minutes per side. Drain on paper towels. Sprinkle with powdered sugar; top with pie filling, if desired. Serve immediately. Makes about 4 servings.

Raspberry-Almond Kuchen

Equally delicious with coffee for brunch or as dessert after dinner.

1 egg, beaten
1/2 c. milk
1/2 c. sugar
2 T. oil
1 t. almond extract

1 c. all-purpose flour
2 t. baking powder
1 c. fresh raspberries
1/2 c. sliced almonds

In a large bowl, combine egg, milk, sugar, oil and extract. Add flour and baking powder; mix well. Spread batter in a greased cast-iron skillet; sprinkle raspberries, Crumb Topping and almonds over batter. Transfer skillet to oven. Bake, uncovered, at 375 degrees for 25 to 30 minutes. Cut into wedges; serve warm. Serves 8.

Crumb Topping:

3/4 c. all-purpose flour
1/2 c. sugar

3 T. chilled butter

Mix flour and sugar; cut in butter with a fork until crumbly.

Prize-Winning Funnel Cakes

Chocolate-Hazelnut Skillet Bars

Chocolate-Hazelnut Skillet Bars

These blondie-like bars are too good to pass up. If you aren't a hazelnut fan, pecans or almonds would be tasty too.

1-1/4 c. all-purpose flour	1 egg, beaten
1/4 t. baking powder	1-1/2 t. vanilla extract
1/2 t. baking soda	1 t. espresso powder
1/2 t. salt	3/4 c. dark baking chocolate,
1/2 c. butter	chopped
1 c. dark brown sugar, packed	1/2 c. hazelnuts, chopped

In a bowl, combine flour, baking powder, baking soda and salt; set aside. Melt butter in a large cast-iron skillet over medium heat. Add brown sugar and whisk until sugar is dissolved, about one minute. Slowly pour butter mixture into flour mixture. Add egg, vanilla and espresso powder to flour mixture; stir until combined. Fold in remaining ingredients. Spoon dough into skillet, flatten gently. Transfer skillet to oven. Bake, uncovered, at 350 degrees for 20 to 25 minutes, until golden on top and a toothpick tests clean. Let stand 30 minutes; slice into wedges to serve. Serves 8.

Glazed Walnuts

These are terrific to snack on. Scoop into jars and add a pretty ribbon for gifts. So good!

1 c. maple syrup	1/2 t. salt
1 T. butter	1 t. vanilla extract
2 t. cinnamon	2 c. walnut halves

In a cast-iron skillet over medium-low heat, cook maple syrup, butter, cinnamon and salt until thickened. Remove from heat; stir in vanilla and walnuts until well coated. Transfer to wax paper-lined baking sheets; allow to cool. Store in a covered container. Makes 2 cups.

Cale's Corn Flake Cookies

*Sweet, crunchy and peanut buttery. An easy
cookie recipe using pantry staples.*

1 c. light corn syrup
1 c. creamy peanut butter
1 c. sugar

1 t. vanilla extract
6 to 7 c. corn flake cereal

In a large cast-iron skillet, combine all ingredients except cereal. Cook and
stir over low heat until smooth. Add cereal; stir well. Drop by tablespoonfuls
onto wax paper. Let stand until cooled and set. Makes 4 dozen.

Skillet Shortcake

*Tender shortcake topped with juicy strawberries...heaven on a plate!
Delicious topped with luscious fresh peaches too.*

2 c. all-purpose flour
1/3 c. sugar
4 t. baking powder
1/2 t. salt
1/8 t. nutmeg
1/2 c. butter, softened and cut into
    chunks

1 egg, well beaten
1/3 c. milk
2 to 3 c. strawberries, hulled and
    sliced
Garnish: whipped cream

In a large bowl, mix flour, sugar, baking powder, salt and nutmeg. Cut in
butter with 2 knives until well blended. Add egg and milk; stir just until
blended, adding a little more milk if needed for dough to hold together.
Spoon dough into a greased cast-iron skillet. Transfer skillet to oven. Bake,
uncovered, at 450 degrees for 15 minutes, or until golden and center tests
done with a toothpick. To serve, cut shortcake into wedges; split wedges
open. Fill with strawberries and top with a dollop of whipped cream.
Serves 6 to 8.

Cale's Corn Flake Cookies

Raised Doughnuts

Raised Doughnuts

There's nothing better on a cool autumn day than sharing warm homemade doughnuts and a mug of crisp cider with friends.

2 c. boiling water
1/2 c. sugar
1 T. salt
2 T. shortening
2 envs. active dry yeast

2 eggs, beaten
7 c. all-purpose flour
oil for frying
Garnish: additional sugar for
    coating

Stir water, sugar, salt and shortening together in a large bowl; sprinkle yeast on top. Set aside; cool to room temperature. Blend in eggs; gradually add flour. Cover and let rise until double in bulk. On a floured surface, roll out dough 1/2-inch thick; cut with a doughnut cutter. Cover doughnuts and let rise again until double in bulk, about 1-1/2 hours. In a skillet, heat 3 inches of oil to 360 degrees. Add doughnuts, a few at a time; fry until golden. Drain on paper towels. Spoon sugar into a paper bag. Add doughnuts and shake to coat. Makes about 4 dozen.

Skillet S'mores

Are the kids begging for s'mores on a rainy day? Let this yummy stovetop recipe come to the rescue.

1 T. butter
10-oz. pkg. mini marshmallows
2 sleeves graham crackers, crushed

2 1-1/2 oz. chocolate candy bars,
    broken into pieces

Melt butter in a cast-iron skillet over medium-low heat. Add marshmallows; stir until completely melted. Remove from heat; stir in graham crackers and chocolate. Press into pan with the back of a spoon. Allow to cool completely; cut into wedges. Makes 10 servings.

Lemon Upside-Down Cake

This elegant sweet-tart cake is sure to be a hit with dinner guests.

4 small lemons, divided	1/2 t. salt
10 T. butter, divided	3/4 c. sugar
3/4 c. light brown sugar, packed	1 t. vanilla extract
1-1/2 c. all-purpose flour	2 eggs
1-1/2 t. baking powder	1/2 c. milk

With a sharp knife, thinly slice 3 lemons, peel and all. Discard any seeds; set aside. From remaining lemon, grate one teaspoon zest; reserve lemon for another use. In a cast-iron skillet, melt 4 tablespoons butter over medium-low heat. Brush bottom and sides of skillet with melted butter. Add brown sugar; stir well and spread evenly in skillet. Arrange lemon slices over the bottom of skillet, slightly overlapping; set aside. Combine flour, baking powder and salt in a bowl. In a separate bowl, beat remaining butter with an electric mixer on medium speed until creamy. Beat in sugar, lemon zest and vanilla until fluffy; beat in eggs, one at a time. Beat in milk and half of flour mixture. Beat in remaining flour mixture. Spread batter evenly over lemon slices in skillet. Transfer skillet to oven. Bake, uncovered, at 350 degrees for 30 to 35 minutes, until golden and center tests done with a toothpick. Cool cake in skillet on a wire rack for 5 minutes. Turn out onto a plate; cut into wedges. Serves 8.

Create a charming cake stand with thrift-store finds. Attach a glass plate with epoxy glue to a short glass vase, tea cup or candle stand for a base. Let dry completely before using...so clever!

Lemon Upside-Down Cake

Toast nuts for extra flavor in recipes...a delicious dessert topping too! Add walnuts, pecans or almonds to a skillet in a single layer. Stir or shake skillet over medium-high heat continually for 5 to 7 minutes. When the nuts start to turn golden and smell toasty, they're done.

Create a heavenly glaze for any apple dessert. Melt together 1/2 cup butterscotch chips, 2 tablespoons butter and 2 tablespoons whipping cream over low heat.

It's simple to save extra whipped cream. Dollop heaping tablespoonfuls onto a chilled baking sheet and freeze. Remove from the baking sheet and store in a plastic zipping bag. To use, place dollops on dessert servings and let stand a few minutes.

For an affordable casual get-together, invite friends over for "just desserts!" Offer a couple of simple homemade desserts like fruit cobblers and crisps, vanilla ice cream for topping and a steamy pot of coffee...they'll love it!

Dutch Ovens & More

Apple Fritter Pancakes

Applesauce replaces some of the oil in these scrumptious pancakes,
so they're a little lighter. Yum!

1 c. all-purpose flour
1/4 t. salt
2 t. baking powder
1 egg, beaten
1 c. milk

1 T. oil
1/2 c. applesauce
1/2 t. nutmeg
1 t. cinnamon-sugar
Garnish: butter, powdered sugar

Combine all ingredients except garnish in a bowl; mix well. Drop batter by 1/4 cupfuls onto a greased cast-iron griddle over medium heat. Turn pancakes when tops start to bubble. Continue to cook until both sides are golden. Serve pancakes topped with butter and powdered sugar. Makes 6 servings.

No time for a leisurely family breakfast? Try serving breakfast for dinner...it's sure to become a family favorite!

Apple Fritter Pancakes

Cranberry Hootycreek Pancakes

Cranberry Hootycreek Pancakes

A delicious breakfast version of a favorite cookie recipe.

1/2 c. all-purpose flour
1/2 c. quick-cooking oats,
　uncooked
1 T. sugar
1 t. baking powder
1/2 t. baking soda
1/2 t. salt

1 t. vanilla extract
3/4 c. buttermilk
2 T. oil
1 egg, beaten
1/2 c. white chocolate chips
1/2 c. sweetened dried cranberries

In a bowl, mix flour, oats, sugar, baking powder, baking soda and salt. Add vanilla, buttermilk, oil and egg; stir until well blended. Stir in chocolate chips and cranberries. Drop batter by 1/4 cupfuls into a lightly greased cast-iron griddle over medium heat. Cook for about 3 minutes, until bubbles start to form on tops. Turn and cook 2 additional minutes, or until both sides are golden. Serves 4.

219

Top warm pancakes with a dollop of maple butter...yum! Just combine 1/2 cup softened butter with 3/4 cup maple syrup and beat until fluffy.

Dilly Chicken Sandwiches

Dutch Ovens & More

Dilly Chicken Sandwiches

This is a great sandwich for a family get-together. Bread & butter pickles make it taste even better!

4 boneless, skinless chicken
  breasts
6 T. butter, softened and divided
1 clove garlic, minced
3/4 t. dill weed, divided

8 slices French bread
4 T. cream cheese, softened
2 t. lemon juice
Garnish: lettuce leaves, tomato
  slices, bread & butter pickles

Place chicken breasts between 2 pieces of wax paper. Using a mallet, flatten to 1/4-inch thickness; set aside. On a cast-iron griddle over medium-high heat, melt 3 tablespoons butter; stir in garlic and 1/2 teaspoon dill weed. Add chicken; cook on both sides until juices run clear. Remove and keep warm. Spread both sides of bread with remaining butter. Wipe griddle clean. Over medium heat, grill bread on both sides until golden. Combine remaining dill weed, cream cheese and lemon juice. Spread on one side of 4 slices grilled bread. Top with chicken; garnish as desired. Top with remaining bread. Makes 4 servings.

221

Apple Gem Cakes

These tasty fruit muffins are named for an old-fashioned cast-iron gem cake pan.

2 c. self-rising flour
1/2 c. sugar
1 c. apple, cored, peeled and finely
  chopped
1 egg, beaten
1 c. milk

3 T. butter, melted and slightly
  cooled
1/3 c. brown sugar, packed
1/2 c. chopped pecans or walnuts
1/2 t. cinnamon

Sift flour and sugar together into a bowl. Add apple; mix well. In a separate bowl, combine egg, milk and butter. Add to flour mixture and stir just enough to moisten. Spoon into a greased cast-iron muffin pan, filling cups 3/4 full. Combine remaining ingredients; sprinkle over batter. Bake at 400 degrees for 15 to 20 minutes. Makes one dozen.

Chili with Corn Dumplings

So simple, yet so satisfying...share it on a chilly night around a campfire.

1-1/2 lbs. ground beef
3/4 c. onion, chopped
15-oz. can corn, drained and liquid
   reserved
16-oz. can stewed tomatoes
16-oz. can tomato sauce
1 t. hot pepper sauce

2 T. chili powder
1 t. garlic, minced
1-1/3 c. biscuit baking mix
2/3 c. cornmeal
2/3 c. milk
3 T. fresh cilantro, chopped

Brown beef and onion in a cast-iron Dutch oven over medium heat; drain. Set aside 1/2 cup corn; stir remaining corn with reserved liquid, tomatoes with juice, sauces, chili powder and garlic into beef mixture. Heat to boiling. Reduce heat; cover and simmer for 15 minutes. Combine biscuit mix and cornmeal in a bowl; stir in milk, cilantro and reserved corn just until moistened. Drop dough by rounded tablespoonfuls onto simmering chili. Cook over low heat, uncovered, for 15 minutes. Cover and cook an additional 15 to 18 minutes, until dumplings are dry on top. Makes 6 servings.

When serving chili, set out a variety of fun toppings...fill bowls with shredded cheese, chopped onions, sour cream and crunchy corn chips, then invite everyone to dig in!

Chili with Corn Dumplings

Aunt Annie's Chicken Paprika

Aunt Annie's Chicken Paprika

A very special dish from the old country.

2 to 3 t. all-purpose flour
1 t. salt
1/4 t. pepper
4 lbs. chicken
oil for frying
3 onions, sliced

1 clove garlic, chopped
6 carrots, peeled and sliced
2 T. Hungarian paprika
2 c. water
3 cubes chicken bouillon
cooked spaetzle or egg noodles

Mix flour, salt and pepper in a plastic zipping bag. Add chicken pieces, 2 at a time; toss to coat. Heat 2 tablespoons oil in a cast-iron Dutch oven over medium-high heat. Sauté onions and garlic until tender; remove from pan and set aside. Add additional oil, about 1/2-inch deep. Add chicken and cook, turning once, until golden on both sides. Remove chicken to a plate. Drain pan; return onion mixture to pan along with carrots, paprika, water and bouillon. Bring to a boil over medium-high heat; return chicken to pan. Reduce heat to low. Cover and simmer for one hour, or until chicken juices run clear. Serve chicken and vegetables with cooked spaetzle or noodles. Makes 8 servings.

Ask family & friends to share a copy of tried & true recipe favorites and create a special cookbook...a great gift for a new cook in the family.

Dijon Beef Stew

A loaf of crusty French bread, a salad of mixed greens and steamy bowls of this stew...what could be better?

1-1/2 lbs. stew beef cubes
1/4 c. all-purpose flour
2 T. oil
salt and pepper to taste
2 14-1/2 oz. cans diced tomatoes
    with garlic and onion

14-1/2 oz. can beef broth
4 carrots, peeled and sliced
2 potatoes, peeled and cubed
3/4 t. dried thyme
2 T. Dijon mustard

Combine beef and flour in a large plastic zipping bag; toss to coat evenly. Add oil to a cast-iron Dutch oven over medium-high heat. Brown beef; season with salt and pepper. Drain; add tomatoes with juice and remaining ingredients except mustard. Bring to a boil; reduce heat to medium-low. Cover and simmer for one hour, or until beef is tender. Stir in mustard. Makes 6 to 8 servings.

Green Pepper Soup

If you like stuffed green peppers, you'll love this hearty soup.

2 lbs. ground beef
28-oz. can diced tomatoes
28-oz. can tomato sauce
2 c. cooked rice

2 c. green peppers, chopped
2 cubes beef bouillon
1/4 c. brown sugar, packed
2 t. pepper

Brown beef in a cast-iron Dutch oven over medium heat; drain. Add tomatoes with juice and remaining ingredients. Bring to a boil. Reduce heat to medium-low; cover and simmer for 30 to 40 minutes, until peppers are tender. Makes 8 to 10 servings.

Take a hike while dinner simmers...bring along some trail mix for munching. Toss together peanuts, raisins, sunflower kernels and fish-shaped crackers and fill some little zipping bags...a lifesaver for growling tummies!

Dijon Beef Stew

Zesty Minestrone

Zesty Minestrone

This delicious soup reheats well...a great make-ahead for tailgate parties!

1 lb. Italian pork sausage links,
  sliced
2 t. oil
1 onion, chopped
1 green pepper, chopped
3 cloves garlic, chopped
28-oz. can whole tomatoes
2 potatoes, peeled and diced
1/4 c. fresh parsley, chopped

2 t. dried oregano
1 t. dried basil
1 t. fennel seed
1/2 t. red pepper flakes
salt and pepper to taste
4 c. beef broth
2 16-oz. cans kidney beans
1 c. elbow macaroni, uncooked

Sauté sausage in oil in a cast-iron Dutch oven over medium heat; drain. Add onion, green pepper and garlic; cook 5 minutes. Add tomatoes with juice, potatoes, seasonings and beef broth; bring to a boil. Reduce heat; simmer for 30 minutes. Stir in undrained beans and uncooked macaroni. Simmer an additional 10 minutes, or until macaroni is tender. Makes 6 to 8 servings.

229

Try packing pita bread, flatbread or tortillas for camping instead of regular loaf bread. They're tasty warmed up on a griddle over the fire and won't crush when packed.

Ham & Bean Soup

Always a welcome meal after a chilly day in the football stands watching the game!

1 c. dried navy beans
8 c. water, divided
2 stalks celery, sliced
2 carrots, peeled and sliced
1 onion, chopped

3/4 c. cooked ham, cubed
1 cube chicken bouillon
1 t. dried thyme
2 bay leaves
1/4 t. pepper

In a cast-iron Dutch oven, combine beans and 4 cups water. Bring to a boil; reduce heat to low. Simmer, uncovered, for 2 minutes. Remove from heat. Cover; let stand for one hour. Drain and rinse beans; return to pan. Add remaining water and other ingredients. Bring to a boil; reduce heat to low. Cover and simmer for 1-1/4 hours, or until beans are tender. Discard bay leaves. Using a fork, slightly mash some of the beans against the side of the pan to thicken soup. Makes 6 to 8 servings.

Pan-Fried Corn Fritters

Delicious with campfire chili or a big kettle of ham & beans!

1 c. biscuit baking mix
8-3/4 oz. can corn, drained
1 egg, beaten

1/4 c. water
1 to 2 T. bacon drippings or oil
Garnish: butter or maple syrup

Combine biscuit mix, corn, egg and water in a bowl; stir well. Grease a cast-iron griddle with drippings or oil. Drop batter onto griddle by 1/4 cupfuls. Cook over medium-low heat for about 5 minutes on each side, until golden. Serve warm with butter or syrup. Makes 6 to 8 fritters.

Dried beans are cheap and tasty, but if you don't have time to soak them, canned beans are an excellent choice too. One pound of dried beans equals 3 to 4 cans of beans. Drain and rinse them well before adding to a recipe.

Ham & Bean Soup

Campers' Beans

Campers' Beans

Sweet and satisfying...almost a meal in itself!

6 to 8 slices bacon
1 onion, chopped
1/4 c. brown sugar, packed
1/4 c. catsup
2 T. mustard

2 t. vinegar
2 32-oz. cans baked beans
Optional: additional crumbled
    bacon

Cook bacon in a cast-iron Dutch oven over medium-high heat. When partially cooked, add onion. Continue cooking until bacon is crisp. Remove bacon and onion to a paper towel; drain pan. To the same pan, add brown sugar, catsup, mustard and vinegar; simmer over low heat for 15 minutes. Stir in beans with liquid, crumbled bacon and onion. Simmer, uncovered, over medium-low heat for at least 30 minutes, stirring often. If desired, garnish with additional bacon. Makes 8 to 10 servings.

233

Choose a crisp fall evening to host a bonfire party. Gather friends of all ages...serve chili, hot cider and s'mores, tell ghost stories and sing songs together. You'll be making memories that will last a lifetime!

Chicken Cacciatore

This delicious recipe is easy to double. Try using Italian-seasoned diced tomatoes for even more flavor.

1 lb. boneless, skinless chicken
  breast, cubed
2 T. oil
14-1/2 oz. can diced tomatoes
28-oz. jar spaghetti sauce
1 green pepper, sliced

1 onion, chopped
2 cloves garlic, minced
1 t. Italian seasoning
salt and pepper to taste
cooked pasta or rice
Garnish: grated Parmesan cheese

In a cast-iron Dutch oven over medium heat, brown chicken in oil. Drain; stir in tomatoes with juice and remaining ingredients except cheese. Reduce heat to medium-low. Cover and simmer until vegetables are tender, stirring occasionally. Serve over cooked pasta or rice, topped with Parmesan cheese. Makes 2 to 4 servings.

234

Warm garlic bread can't be beat! Mix 1/2 cup melted butter and two teaspoons minced garlic; spread over a split loaf of Italian bread. Sprinkle with chopped fresh parsley. Bake at 350 degrees for eight minutes, or until hot, then broil briefly, until golden. Cut into generous slices.

Chicken Cacciatore

Delicious Pot Roast

Delicious Pot Roast

You can't beat an old fashioned pot roast with all the trimmings... just like Grandma used to make.

4-lb. boneless beef chuck roast
2 cloves garlic, thinly sliced
1/4 c. all-purpose flour
1/2 t. salt
1/2 t. pepper
1/3 c. olive oil
1 onion, sliced
1 c. red wine or beef broth
8-oz. can tomato sauce

1 T. brown sugar, packed
1 t. prepared horseradish
1 t. mustard
1 t. dried oregano
1 bay leaf
8 new red potatoes
6 carrots, peeled and quartered
4 stalks celery, sliced

With a knifetip, cut small slits in the top of roast; insert a slice of garlic into each slit. Dredge roast in flour; season with salt and pepper. Heat oil in a cast-iron Dutch oven over medium heat. Brown roast on all sides. Add onion and wine or beef broth to pan. Combine tomato sauce, brown sugar, horseradish, mustard, oregano and bay leaf in a bowl; spoon over roast. Bring to a boil; reduce heat to medium-low. Cover and simmer for 1-1/2 hours. Arrange vegetables around roast. Cover and cook for one more hour. Remove roast to a serving platter; let stand for 10 minutes before slicing. Discard bay leaf. Serve roast topped with pan juices. Serves 8.

237

German-Style Short Ribs

*The kitchen will smell warm and delicious when these ribs
are simmering on the stove.*

2 T. oil
3 lbs. beef short ribs
10-1/2 oz. can French onion soup
1 c. water
1 T. lemon juice

1/4 t. ground cloves
1/4 t. pepper
2 to 3 slices pumpernickel bread,
   crumbled
cooked rice or egg noodles

Heat oil in a cast-iron Dutch oven over medium heat. Brown ribs on all
sides for 6 to 8 minutes; drain. Add soup, water, lemon juice and spices;
bring to a boil. Cover and reduce heat to low. Simmer for 1-1/2 to 2 hours,
stirring occasionally. Stir in bread crumbs. Serve ribs and gravy ladled over
cooked rice or noodles. Serves 4.

Granny's Campfire Special

*This meal is all in one pot and so easy to fix! Just serve it with cornbread
or biscuits, then sit back and watch everyone eat it up.*

1 to 2 lbs. ground beef chuck
salt and pepper to taste
1 sweet onion, sliced and separated
   into rings

6 to 8 potatoes, peeled and thinly
   sliced
1 head cabbage, coarsely chopped
Optional: baby carrots

Crumble beef loosely into a cast-iron Dutch oven; season with salt and
pepper. Arrange onion rings and potato slices over beef; season with more
salt and pepper. Place cabbage over potatoes; top with carrots, if using.
Cover and simmer over medium heat for about 45 minutes, until beef is no
longer pink and potatoes are tender. Makes 6 to 8 servings.

German-Style Short Ribs

Savory Cheese & Bacon Potatoes

Savory Cheese & Bacon Potatoes

These cheesy mashed potatoes are out of this world!

2-1/2 lbs. Yukon Gold potatoes,
   peeled and quartered
3 T. butter, softened
2-1/2 c. mixed shredded cheeses,
   such as Swiss, Italian and
   casserole style
1/2 to 3/4 c. milk, warmed

4 slices bacon, crisply cooked and
   crumbled
2 t. dried sage
salt and pepper to taste
Optional: additional shredded
   cheese

Cover potatoes with water in a cast-iron Dutch oven. Bring to a boil; cook until tender, 15 to 18 minutes. Drain potatoes; return to warm pan and mash. Blend in butter and cheeses; add enough milk to make a creamy consistency. Stir in crumbled bacon and seasonings. Sprinkle with additional cheese, if desired. Makes 8 servings.

Cheese tends to turn crumbly when frozen...fine to use in baked dishes like Savory Cheese & Bacon Potatoes. Stock up when cheese is on sale and thaw overnight in the refrigerator before using.

Lucky-7 Mac & Cheese

Wow! This homestyle favorite has seven kinds of cheese...sure to be the cheesiest, tastiest mac & cheese you've ever had.

16-oz. pkg. elbow macaroni,
  uncooked
1 c. milk
1/2 c. extra-sharp Cheddar cheese,
  diced
1/2 c. Colby cheese, diced
1/2 c. pasteurized process cheese
  spread, diced

1/2 c. Swiss cheese, diced
1/2 c. provolone cheese, diced
1/2 c. Monterey Jack cheese, diced
1/2 c. crumbled blue cheese
salt and pepper to taste

Cook macaroni according to package directions; drain. Meanwhile, in a cast-iron Dutch oven, combine milk and cheeses. Cook over medium-low heat until melted, stirring often. Fold in cooked macaroni until coated well; season with salt and pepper. Heat through over low heat, stirring occasionally. Makes 6 to 8 servings.

Do you love a crunchy golden crumb topping on your stovetop mac & cheese? Toss some soft fresh bread crumbs with a little melted butter and sizzle them in a skillet until toasty.

Lucky-7 Mac & Cheese

BBQ Pork Ribs

BBQ Pork Ribs

Pair these juicy ribs with a big platter of corn on the cob.

3 qts. water	1 onion, quartered
4 lbs. pork ribs, cut into serving- size portions	2 t. salt 1/4 t. pepper

Bring water to a boil in a cast-iron Dutch oven over high heat. Add ribs, onion, salt and pepper. Reduce heat to medium-low. Cover and simmer for 1-1/2 hours, or until ribs are tender, stirring occasionally. Prepare BBQ Sauce while ribs are simmering. Remove ribs to a platter; drain and discard cooking liquid. Grill or broil ribs for 10 minutes on each side, brushing often with BBQ Sauce, until sauce is caramelized. Serves 4 to 6.

BBQ Sauce:

1/2 c. vinegar	1/2 c. brown sugar, packed
1 T. lemon juice	1/2 t. dry mustard
1/2 c. chili sauce	1/8 t. garlic powder
1/4 c. Worcestershire sauce	1/8 t. cayenne pepper
2 T. onion, chopped	

Combine all ingredients in a small saucepan. Simmer over low heat for 30 minutes, stirring often.

Serve up a salad topped with grilled apple slices...yummy with pears too! Heat a tablespoon each of olive oil and maple syrup in a skillet. Add thin slices of tart apple. Cook for 6 to 8 minutes, turning once, until deep golden and crisp. Serve warm.

Dutch Oven Peach Cobbler

An old camping favorite! Very easy to do and the results are delicious!

29-oz. can sliced peaches, drained
1-1/2 c. sugar, divided
1 t. butter, melted
1 c. all-purpose flour
2 t. baking powder
1/2 t. salt
1/2 c. milk
1/2 c. water

Place peaches in a greased cast-iron Dutch oven; set aside. In a bowl, mix 1/2 cup sugar and butter. In a separate bowl, mix flour, baking powder and salt. Stir flour mixture and milk into sugar mixture. Pour batter over peaches. Sprinkle with remaining sugar; pour water over batter without stirring. Cover Dutch oven with lid. Bake at 350 degrees for one hour, or until bubbly and golden. Serve warm. Makes 6 to 8 servings.

Campfire Directions:

Prepare a campfire with plenty of hot charcoal briquets. Place peaches in a greased cast-iron Dutch oven; set near fire to warm. Prepare batter and add to peaches; add remaining sugar and water as described above. Arrange 7 hot charcoal briquets in a ring; set Dutch oven on top. Add lid; place 14 briquets on lid. Cook for about one hour. Every 15 minutes, carefully rotate Dutch oven 1/4 turn to the right and rotate lid 1/4 turn to the left; replace briquets on lid as needed. Cobbler is done when bubbly and golden.

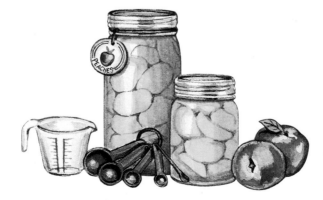

Enjoy a homestyle dessert like Dutch Oven Peach Cobbler in front of a crackling fireplace...pure comfort!

Dutch Oven Peach Cobbler

Raisin Griddle Cake Cookies

Raisin Griddle Cake Cookies

These are so easy...just mix, roll, cut and cook on a griddle. So fast when company is coming. These cookies store well, but they won't last long!

1-1/4 c. raisins	1 t. salt
2 c. hot water	1 t. nutmeg
3-1/2 c. all-purpose flour	1 c. butter-flavored shortening
1 c. sugar	1 egg, beaten
1-1/2 t. baking powder	1/2 c. milk
1/2 t. baking soda	oil for griddle

Combine raisins and hot water in a bowl; set aside. In a large bowl, mix flour, sugar, baking powder, baking soda, salt and nutmeg. Cut in shortening with 2 knives until crumbly. In a small bowl, whisk together egg and milk; add to dough. Drain raisins and add to dough. Stir to form a slightly stiff but smooth dough. Roll out dough on a floured surface to 1/4-inch thick. Cut out dough with a round biscuit cutter. Heat a griddle over medium heat until a drop of water dances on the griddle. Oil griddle lightly. Add cookies, several at a time. Cook for several minutes, until lightly golden on bottom; turn and cook other side. Cool cookies on a wire rack. Dough may also be rolled into a log shape, wrapped in wax paper or plastic wrap and frozen. Thaw, slice and bake as needed. Makes about one dozen large cookies or 2 dozen small cookies.

Jams, jellies and preserves keep well, so stock up on homemade local specialties whenever you travel. They'll be scrumptious on breakfast muffins and dinner rolls.

Lemony Blackberry Crisp

The perfect reward for an afternoon spent picking blackberries!

5 c. fresh or frozen blackberries
1/4 c. sugar
2 T. cornstarch
3 T. lemon juice
25 vanilla wafers, crushed
1/2 c. old-fashioned oats,
   uncooked

1/2 c. light brown sugar, packed
1/4 c. all-purpose flour
1/2 t. cinnamon
1/2 c. butter, melted
Garnish: vanilla ice cream

Place blackberries in a cast-iron Dutch oven; sprinkle with sugar and set aside. In a cup, stir together cornstarch and lemon juice; add to berries and mix gently. In a bowl, combine vanilla wafer crumbs, oats, brown sugar, flour and cinnamon. Add butter; stir until crumbly. Sprinkle crumb mixture over berries. Bake, uncovered, at 400 degrees for 25 to 30 minutes, until bubbly and lightly golden. Serve warm, topped with a scoop of ice cream. Makes 4 to 6 servings.

Serve up cobbler parfaits in mini Mason jars, just for fun. Alternate scoops of fruit cobbler or crisp and layers of ice cream. Garnish with whipped topping and a sprig of fresh mint.

Lemony Blackberry Crisp

Get your campfire started and ready for cooking quickly! Crumple newspaper for the first layer, then add dry twigs. Light the paper, add wood and let it burn until you get red glowing coals. Let it burn down a bit more, then place the cooking grate over the coals.

Camp cooking is super-easy when you chop or shred veggies and cheese at home, then pack in plastic zipping bags and place in a cooler. Don't chop potatoes or apples ahead of time, though, as they'll darken before being cooked.

Host a chili cook-off! Ask neighbors to bring a pot of their "secret recipe" chili to share, then have a friendly judging for the best. You can even hand out wooden spoons, oven mitts and aprons as prizes!

On the way to your campsite, if you see a sign for a tag or barn sale, don't pass it by! You're sure to find oodles of ideas for bringing whimsy to your garden back home. You may even find old cast-iron pans that can be put to use in your kitchen!

Index

Index

Index

Sides

Soups & Stews

sizzling skillets

campfire treats

fried pies

Granny's kitchen

Dutch oven delights

cozy dinners

bubbling cobblers

hearty stews

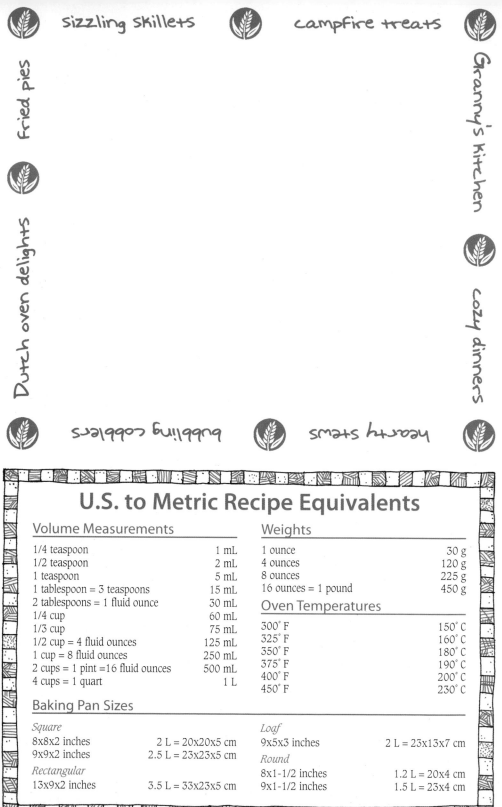

U.S. to Metric Recipe Equivalents

Volume Measurements

1/4 teaspoon	1 mL
1/2 teaspoon	2 mL
1 teaspoon	5 mL
1 tablespoon = 3 teaspoons	15 mL
2 tablespoons = 1 fluid ounce	30 mL
1/4 cup	60 mL
1/3 cup	75 mL
1/2 cup = 4 fluid ounces	125 mL
1 cup = 8 fluid ounces	250 mL
2 cups = 1 pint =16 fluid ounces	500 mL
4 cups = 1 quart	1 L

Weights

1 ounce	30 g
4 ounces	120 g
8 ounces	225 g
16 ounces = 1 pound	450 g

Oven Temperatures

300° F	150° C
325° F	160° C
350° F	180° C
375° F	190° C
400° F	200° C
450° F	230° C

Baking Pan Sizes

Square

8x8x2 inches	2 L = 20x20x5 cm
9x9x2 inches	2.5 L = 23x23x5 cm

Rectangular

13x9x2 inches	3.5 L = 33x23x5 cm

Loaf

9x5x3 inches	2 L = 23x13x7 cm

Round

8x1-1/2 inches	1.2 L = 20x4 cm
9x1-1/2 inches	1.5 L = 23x4 cm